## What Others Are

In *Rape to Righteousness,* Charlie Coker has been willing to be so vulnerable with his story in order for so many to reconcile theirs. He has done an amazing job of defining, explaining, and comparing natural violations and abuses to those spiritual violations and abuses found in homes, communities, and even safe places like schools and houses of worship. He is an excellent storyteller, and God has given this man the opportunity and ability to tell his story in such a compelling way that people feel invited, safe, and free to share their own. You will not only be blessed, wrecked, informed, and enlightened by this book and all it brings to the table, but the greatest aspect of it is that you will engage in something of a deliverance from mindsets that may have tormented you or others you know and love for years. This book will set you (and them) on a trajectory of life, hope, freedom, and purpose without the weight of guilt, shame, or condemnation anchoring you or others; and as a result, it will propel you into a momentum of abundant life that you may have never known before. So strap in, put on your non-offended prescription reading glasses, be at peace and rest, and be free to think differently about God, yourself, and others. Enjoy the ride!

**— Scott Lowmaster**
   Senior Leader Journey Church, President and Founder of the Journey Center,
   Journey Academy, and the iMatter Foundation and Festival

Few words are necessary in introducing a book like this one. When you open its pages you will understand why. This book is vintage Charlie Coker: to-the-point and bare-knuckles in language and in-your-face with obvious and inarguable conclusions. Charlie and Susie Coker have seen it all, and this book opens mysteries few would dare to discuss with anyone. Both of these very remarkable people have faced the past and dealt properly with it so as to be able to reveal, through their marriage, the power of innocence and the sheer delight of honesty and openness. Waves of revelation will surely accompany and follow the reading of the following pages.

You are about to enter the adventure of a shocking story well told. Store it in a place in your mind where you will be moved to enjoy and benefit from the principles learned in the laboratory of stubborn love. If you are looking for a tragedy of epic proportions, coupled with and crowned by a resounding victory of the miraculous and unforgettable features of the dual power of love that refused to let go, along with undaunted faith, you have come to the right address! Come right in and help yourself and read on. Blessings and benefits await you!

— **Jack Taylor, President**
  Dimensions Ministries, Melbourne, Florida

If honest, transparency, and courage were enough, this book would shift the body of Christ. Charlie's and Susie's willingness to share their transformational journey is drastically humbling. But that is not enough. Depth of understanding, revelation from heaven, wisdom, and an experience to make God's severe redemption a reality are added in heaps to make this book one that removes the chains that bar healing. Today, Charlie and Susie Coker stand tall and cut a wide swath in the kingdom. This book is proof positive that if you are willing, nothing can stop His redeeming love.

— **Brian Higbee**
  Author and Senior Leader of CityChurch, Connellsville, Pennsylvania

Charlie Coker has written a timely book that clearly gives a message of how to heal from abuse. His story shows how love and forgiveness are eternal truths that give freedom from self-hate to both the abused and the abuser.

— **Beverly C. Brim, M.A.**
  Licensed Mental Health Counselor

Openly candid and extremely transparent, this is one book I'll never forget. Read this unforgettable true story of how grace and forgiveness can really work in the lives of several ordinary, messed-up people.

— **Dr. Andy Sanders**
  Author and Evangelist

*From*

# RAPE

*to*
# Righteousness

*Redeeming the Bride of Christ*

# CHARLIE COKER

Printed in the United States of America

ISBN: 978-1-7330786-1-0

# Dedication

I dedicate this book to the ones I love the most:

Susie Coker—thank you for putting up with me over the years.

My sons, Jason and Bryan, and all of my accountability partners who have been most valuable in keeping me on my walk with God.

To Papa Jack Taylor. Without your love and relationship, I would still have major issues with a false identity.

I must thank all of people who make up Identity Church. Without your prayers and love, this journey would have not happened.

# Acknowledgments

I would like to thank my wife, Susie Coker, for all of her hard work in assisting me in getting this book ready to publish.

I would also like to thank the editors, graphic artist, and production team for getting this long-running (seemingly never-ending) project through to print and into all of the hands of those who will be reading this book.

Last but not least, I would like to give a special thank-you to my writing coach, who has patiently worked with me. You have a God-given talent in helping people like me take their book to a whole new level. You have really taught me a lot about the importance of being committed to writing.

You all have done an outstanding job! Thank you!

— Charlie Coker

# Contents

# Contents

# Foreword

C harlie Coker is one of the best revelators I know. If you know Charlie, and you've ever heard him speak, you known that you're always on the edge of your seat with this feeling in your gut that anything could happen right now. Further, you know that the "anything" could change your life forever. Beyond having merely a comprehensive grasp of the Scriptures, it becomes clear very quickly that Charlie is very close to the Author. Because of his intrepid nature, I wasn't surprised when he decided to write his story. With a fearless vulnerability, this book gives language to a situation that, for many, is unthinkable. And yet, for many others, it is an inescapable part of their own story. Far beyond merely being shocking in its subject matter, this book contains some of the best revelation on the healing power of grace that I've ever seen or heard. If the measure of *grace one has received* reveals the measure of *love one carries*, then Charlie and Susie Coker have grace enough to give away for eternity!

There are two parts of this book that impressed me the most. The first part is the sections at the close of each chapter, called "How Does This Apply to the Church?" The messages found in these are extremely important: far beyond being a personal memoir of a dark season. Every pastor would do well to step into this story because if you've been in ministry for very long, you've seen some stuff. To hear from both the victim and the abuser who have both walked through this together, and come out pointing to the resurrecting and redeeming power of Jesus Christ as the One who brings wholeness: well, that's a revelation you need to get.

The second part that I found invaluable was Susie's perspective. How often do we get to hear both sides of the story? When a grace-fueled victim steps into the conversation, the narrative is lifted beyond mere right and wrong and into the revelation of redemption and restoration. Clearly, Susie is no longer a victim, but an empowered daughter whose intentional release of grace changes Charlie's identity too. These dual perspectives make this book uniquely personal and appealing to a wide variety of people. If you've been an abuser, hearing from Charlie will give you hope in the reconciling power of Christ to not just reclaim your life and redeem your past, but restore your reputation as well. If you've been a victim, hearing from Susie will give you an empowered understanding that in Christ you are whole and complete and far stronger than you could possibly imagine. If you're a pastor or leader, hearing from the Cokers will give you a resource that will speak to the most broken people in your care and reveal exactly what God can do with a situation that seems devoid of hope.

Revelation that comes from experience, and understanding in which love is the final word, is a rare treasure indeed. Charlie and Susie are treasures of hope, generals of grace, and champions of the finished work of the cross. The last few chapters alone carry enough revelation to make the book well worth the investment of time you're about to take. Through hearing the Cokers' story I've come to believe that our Father is not just a forgiver; He is a restorer of innocence. May you be baptized in the innocence of Jesus Christ as you read this powerful book.

**— Bill Vanderbush**
Author and Pastor of Community Presbyterian Church in Celebration, Florida

Above all, love each other
deeply, because love covers
over a multitude of sins.

(1 Peter 4:8)

# Preface

I've had many people ask me how I can stand up and publicly tell the story about being raped and then becoming the one who raped—the rapist. They wonder why I am not ashamed. Well, that answer is simple: The true gospel of the kingdom starts with forgiveness, moves to innocence, and then to holiness.

> To be made new in the attitude of your minds; and to put on the new self, created to be like God in true righteousness and holiness. Therefore each of you must put off falsehood and speak truthfully to your neighbor, for we are all members of one body. (Ephesians 4:23–25)

Leaving an old life of sin and shame and taking on the new life through Jesus Christ, where there isn't any condemnation, is holiness. Holiness is living free—without guilt—being made innocent. Holiness is *not* based on the outward appearance, but the internal transformation of the heart instead. Learning how to live holy is impossible without the blood of Jesus. Why? Only Christ can transform the inner workings of a person's heart. In other words, He can take the worst of sinners on earth and transform them to become free—and holy. This is because His blood takes away the shame, and this is what He did for me several years ago.

When I first started walking with Jesus, I was battling all the perversions and residual effects of my former sin life and crying out to the Lord for relief in my mind. (Keep in mind that that there are always residual effects of sin and consequences from it. There are many on death row who have found forgiveness of sins through the blood of Jesus, but they are still in jail because they killed someone. Coming to Christ doesn't mean this life is instantly fixed from our consequences. Sometimes we have to walk them out.)

At this time I had a vision: I was sitting at the bottom of the cross with Jesus hanging on it. As I looked up at Him, I saw that His side was pierced and blood was running down his thighs, past the calves, all the way to his big toe. As I looked up, I saw one drop of His blood leave His toe and land on the top of my head. Immediately, peace covered my soul. Instantly, I found an internal harmony in my mind and divine rest for my soul. At that exact moment, the Lord said to me, "Did you notice that I was naked and that I am circumcised? My life, My blood, not only took away your sin but also your shame. I took away all of the world's shame. My death, My blood, on the cross took away your sins and your shame—both. I was naked, and I took the shame of your past away." When He said that to me, and I grasped the depths of His love and what He went through to set us free, you and me, I never doubted this again. From that moment on, I haven't been ashamed of my past life. Jesus took my shame away.

In Jesus's time, being exposed and completely naked was the worst thing that could ever happen to a person. Public humiliation was the worst form of shame someone could ever have, and Christ endured it for you and for me.

When this happened to Him, He took away our shame and the public humiliation for our sins. As I realized this, Christ said to me, "I was naked, balls and all!" Jesus Christ went through the worst form of shame and humiliation in order to release the redeeming power of God on His bride. Without His nakedness and His shame, we would not be free today.

What you are about to read is a book seasoned with love, yet direct in nature. This is a book written to help set people free from the tragedies of rape and the effects of it. Sexual assault is rampant in our culture. It is at an all-time high. This book is written to help free both the woman and the man in some of the most private and personal areas of life.

# Introduction

There's an article that's sure to grab the attention of most readers immediately. For some it will strike a painful spot deep within their own heart.

It's a sad story about a fifteen-year-old girl who decided to go to her high school prom. For the most part she wasn't a troublemaker; she wasn't out of touch with a typical high schooler's lifestyle. On her prom night, a special time when young girls dress up and spend hours (even days) getting ready, this young girl did just that. She prepped, got prettied up, and off she went to enjoy a fun night at her prom with some of her friends.

While she was at the prom, she had some alcohol. (Isn't it interesting how alcohol opens so many doors to tragedy?) Unfortunately, this young lady never made it from the building back to her dad's care that night. What was supposed to have been a fun night quickly turned into her worst nightmare—something that she will remember and have to cope with for the rest of her life. As she was walking out of the high school gymnasium and heading toward the drop-off and pick-up area to meet her dad, she was approached by another classmate near the courtyard of the school campus to drink a little more alcohol with a group of people before she got picked up. She decided to go ahead for a few more rounds of booze while she waited for her dad.

Over the next few hours, she was brutally beaten and raped over and over again by somewhere close to six or more high school teenagers, including some older out-of-high-school friends that were in the group. Eventually she was let go and, finally, someone had the guts to notify

17

the police; the authorities later found this nearly unconscious girl near a picnic table on the school property. The attack had been so violent that one report stated that the wounds on her body depicted nothing less than dehumanization. The bottom line was that she was literally tortured for two full hours. This all took place on high school property while people walked past on the other side of the courtyard, through the school grass, and on nearby sidewalks. They all chose to do nothing. They looked away and went to the prom or home with their parents and friends.[1]

The school police and administrators who were there that night had all been monitoring the prom from inside the gym. Not one of them walked the perimeters of the school property the entire night.

*So why this story about a fifteen-year-old girl who none of us have ever met?*

Well, that's a simple question to answer: this type of story, believe it or not, happens all the time. For many of you reading this, sexual abuse (rape) happens more than what you probably realize.

One statistic suggests that one in six women have had a near-rape experience or have been raped in their lifetime.[2]

Sexual attacks affect everyone. They aren't just overseas in some far-off, war-torn country. No, this evil is right here—in our own schools, neighborhoods, and communities. And don't forget about the churches too! Tragically, under some circumstances, it is happening right next door or, worse yet, within the trusted walls and structures of our own homes.

Though this book isn't about this girl's specific story, it is about sexual abuse. This is something that is far more common than we realize.

---

1. Associated Press, "Girl Gang-Raped for Two Hours at Homecoming Dance - While a Dozen People Watched and Did Nothing," *New York Daily News,* January 11, 2019, accessed May 02, 2019, http://www.nydailynews.com/news/national/girl-gang-raped-hours-homecoming-dance-dozen-people-watched-article-1.385075.

2. "Scope of the Problem: Statistics," RAINN, accessed May 02, 2019, https://www.rainn.org/statistics/scope-problem.

# INTRODUCTION

Whether you're the victim or the perpetrator, what you are about to read will change your life.

How do you talk about a topic that has haunted you for decades, something that has taken most of your life to process? To make it even more complex, it's a topic that I really don't like discussing and don't want to talk about.

*What's the topic?* Rape!

Rape has been around since the beginning of civilization, and it gets worse in each generation. It will probably never go away until the Lord returns.

Common sense tells us what rape is, but before we go any further, let's take a look at the actual definition of the word *rape* so that we are all on the same page.

Rape is defined as "unlawful sexual activity and usually sexual intercourse carried out forcibly or under threat of injury against a person's will or with a person who is beneath a certain age or incapable of valid consent because of mental illness, mental deficiency, intoxication, unconsciousness, or deception."[3]

Rape or sexual assault is a very serious topic. It's one that nobody should take lightly. If you have never dealt with it yourself, you may never understand what someone has gone or is going through when they have been violently attacked.

One of the things I have learned over the years in dealing with this issue is that sexual assault has little to do with sex—it is mostly about power and control over a victim. It comes from self-hate inside the abuser who is dumping it on the victim by using a sexual act. The assault is designed to humiliate, shame, and make the victim powerless. From this, the abuser gets a temporary feeling of superiority. This feeling does not last long, so they continually look for other victims. We have all heard it said before: Hurt people hurt people.

---

3. "Rape," *Merriam-Webster Dictionary* (online), accessed May 02, 2019, https://www.merriam-webster.com/dictionary/rape.

One online statistic about rape attacks suggest that an American is sexually attacked every ninety-eight seconds.[4]

That is a lot of attacks per hour!

How does this statistic affect you? Every day you walk out your front door, you come into contact with people who have dealt with rape. Maybe you just met someone who was dealing with this from a recent attack. That fifteen-year-old girl didn't know that making the decision to drink a few more rounds of alcohol was going to put her in a horrifying situation over the next two hours. I mean, let's face it: people don't wake up each day assuming that one wrong decision is going to get them raped. It doesn't work like that.

Is the young girl who lives on your street and walks right past your home every school-day morning a reoccurring victim? Is she unable to find safety within her own home? Or is she living in a safe home now, but one day in the near future will she find herself in the wrong place at the wrong time? And at that time, because of a violent rape, her life will be destroyed forever.

What about the "rough-cut" man you stand next to every afternoon while you work in the factory? Is he just another jerk that you have to deal with … or is he a victim of assault, of something that happened long ago: a memory he has learned to suppress, a deep pain he has avoided? He lives the way he does so that absolutely nobody will ever harm him again. He even goes so far as to force all three of his kids to go through martial arts in order to give himself a greater peace of mind, in case one of them gets thrown into the same situation he was in. His kids will be able to get out of it, or at least put up a fight, in a way that their attacker will know to never try it again.

Tragedy can strike at any time, regardless of whether you are a Christian. Sexual attacks can happen against anyone. God knows this. He knows that our plans, dreams, and, in some ways, our lives can

---

4. "Scope of the Problem: Statistics," RAINN, accessed May 02, 2019, https://www.rainn.org/statistics/scope-problem.

instantly—and without warning—be completely crushed. This is why He has places scriptures like this in the book of Psalms:

> The Lord is near to the brokenhearted and saves the crushed in spirit. (Psalm 34:18 ESV)

Most who fall victim to rape do nothing about it; they go home, clean up, go to their rooms, and try to physically and emotionally heal all alone. They are never able to cope with what happened or get the help they need.

Rape is so horrifying that the person can't just turn the memories off like we turn off our televisions before bed at night. If the tragedy of sexual abuse has happened to you, what do you do now? How does God help you overcome something that isn't overcome-able? And, last but not least, what do *rape,* and the current state of the church have to do with anything? We are going to answer these questions and some others in the next several pages of this book. At the end of this book we are also going to look at the parallel between what God is doing to release and raise up godly women on the earth and the Me-Too movement.

# Chapter 1: Setting the Stages of Life the Best Way Possible

When the topic of rape is brought up, I am often asked a question about what type of home life I had. Did the family I grew up in somehow create this type of behavior in me? The answer to the last question is *no*. I was born on June 22, 1959, in Vero Beach, Florida. I have spent most of my life right there in that great state nearly surrounded by water. I didn't bounce around from state to state like a military kid does, nor did I spend my time in and out of foster care like many do. Some kids spend a large percentage of their early years as missionary kids off in some foreign country that they know little about. That wasn't me.

What was my childhood like? It is important that you understand this, as it sets the stage for what we will be discussing further on in the book.

My dad was born in 1928. He was in the navy and he was a "man's man." At around 240 pounds, he was aggressive. He was a really hard worker, and he nearly worked himself to death with three jobs to provide for his family: my three older sisters and me. He worked at the post office and owned a lawn-spraying business and a stamp shop all at once. He wasn't a heavy smoker or drinker, and he wasn't into heavy cussing once he became born again, so there wasn't anything like that going on in our home.

We had some arguments, like everyone else did. One time I got tired of him and he got tired of me. But on one occasion, I took him to the ground. The funny thing about it was that when I got him to the ground, he said to me, "Boy, don't let me kill you!" My thought was *Oh! #@!*! What do I do now?* I pinned him on the ground next to the house, and I realized real fast that I could not hold him forever. Dad told me to never let him up because he was going to kick my ass when he caught me; I finally had to let him up, and I ran as fast as I could. He chased me for about two miles and then kicked my butt.

My dad was also a strong leader in the church. We were in church a lot. My parents were always there, helping out and serving the Lord. Once my father got born again, my parents eventually became members of the first Pentecostal church in Indian River County. Eventually, I became a deacon's kid. Whether we were inside or outside the church, my dad placed tough demands on all of us. Heck, even my older sisters were tough!

To help you understand my father a little better, let me tell you a story about him when he was sixty-seven years old. He was fishing with me and some of my friends. We got back to the dock and began unloading the boat. All of a sudden, this boat with two adults and a ten-year-old boy came toward us. He was coming in way too fast because he was drunk. My dad was trying to reach out to keep the drunken guy's boat from banging into our boat, but slam against the dock instead. Because of the speed of the other boat, there was still some banging and clashing between the boats. The drunk guy started yelling at my dad, calling him an old man and telling him he was going to kick his ass. He got in my father's face, and my father said this: "Son, I don't know where you're from, but where I come from it's never one side. If you want to get this started, let's get it on!" I remember my dad speaking to the drunken man and then standing right up where he was. When my dad stood up and showed that guy that he wasn't scared of him, the man backed down real quick. My dad just wasn't the type of person who would back down.

Growing up, there was only one thing about my dad that I didn't like much or understand. I felt like he had a weakness: a fear of man. Many times, what looked like toughness was actually rooted in fear.

He worried about people's opinion of his character. This would play an important role in the type of person I eventually became.

My mom was born in 1924. In her early years, my mother had some very godly roots. My mother was a Christian teenager who had several encounters with the Lord. From around twelve or thirteen years of age, she served the Lord. This story will give you an idea of the level of faith she walked in at a young age. After high school, she walked into a Bible school and right into the dean's office and said to him, "The Lord said to tell you that I'm the one that He was telling you about." The dean of this Bible college had already been prepared by the Lord that someone was coming to the school who couldn't afford it and that God would point them out. Sometime after God spoke to him, my mom walked in and said that to him. She got her tuition paid! This is the power of God at work in a person's life.

Later in life, when I was ten years old, my mother went back to college to get her master's degree in teaching. It was a hard time for me at that age. She was not home much of the time, and I missed her. I only got to see her on the weekends, and Dad was the parent at this time. However, my dad worked his main job at the post office and had two side businesses. I was a momma's boy, so that left me with my sisters, who had no problem using me as a punching bag.

Growing up with parents coming from that era in life (1920s and 1930s) was sometimes tough on kids, but as a family we managed to survive. Even with my dad having three different jobs, we were still considered lower-middle class. We definitely weren't rich or anything like that. My dad made sure that we got to go on one family vacation each year, but that was it.

I was the typical kid growing up. In that day and in my neighborhood, we all played and had fun, doing things like build forts. As I got a little older I also played baseball, football, and loved riding horses. Eventually, my dad worked really hard to buy me a motorcycle. Of course I nearly killed myself on it! I was exposed to both cultures in our community because I owned a horse and was part redneck-country boy, and also was in the beach crowd in Florida.

As I got older, the cute little girls we all played with in the yard didn't look like girls to me anymore; they looked like grown beauties, candy to the eyes! All those fort-building buddies that I once played with quickly put their sticks and shovels down and picked up Playboy magazines, and so did I.

Of course, I was a "deacon's kid," so I had to live up to that. By the time I got to the eleventh grade I was skipping school, normally at someone else's house, and hanging out with my friends and good-looking high school girls. I was missing so much school that there was no way I would have graduated. I eventually made a deal with the school and got my GED. In time, pornography, skipping school, and all of that stuff led to trying drugs. I ended up getting caught and went to jail for about four days. Of course, my dad was just going to leave me there. Thank God for moms! She came and picked me up, brought me home, and told my dad, "You are *not* going to leave my kid in jail!" That was the end of that mess. Once in jail, I was officially branded—branded by the world and marked by the church.

There was nothing that my dad or mom ever did to me or any of my sisters that would have opened the door to some of the tragedy that I am going to experience later. My father and mother never abused any of us. They weren't perfect, but overall, they were really good parents.

Unfortunately, some of you reading this carry a much different story growing up—one filled with abuse and all kinds of bad situations with people who were supposed to protect you, provide for you, and not intentionally hurt you as a child. People who were supposed to be safe. It doesn't matter how or why sexual abuse (rape) occurs; what matters is the fact that it happened. Now it has to be healed.

God is working to both heal the people of God from trauma like rape and also heal the church from spiritual rape, which is forced submission without relationship. We are going to cover both topics (physical and spiritual) as we move further along in this book.

God is working to not only heal people from physical trauma like rape, but He also wants to heal the church. Because I am a pastor, I am not only concerned about physical rape of the body but also spiritual rape that happens to believers when religious churches enforce their power and control over people instead of teaching members to have a relationship with Jesus. Both are acts of destruction that can damage a person's soul.

# Chapter 2: What You Don't Know Can Hurt You!

I f we attempted to go back and clean everything up in life that our ancestors did, we would be cleaning something up every minute of the day. Some things are better just left alone. There are other things that we need to go back and fix. There are some sins that create a momentary mess, but there are other sins that can haunt a bloodline for a long time (1 John 5:16).

Before we go any further, I think it is worth mentioning a few things that I have discovered in my bloodline. While you are reading this section, it might be good to pray about what you might not know about concerning the history of your family. Be careful and take this seriously, though, because you may start to find some shocking facts that you never knew.

With the new technology in DNA testing, there are many hidden stories about people's pasts now coming into the light, bringing unknown truths to many of our pasts. A friend of mine was recently contacted by a person who claimed, through DNA testing, that they were actually close cousins. This brought an interesting scenario into my friend's family because how do you accidently miss a close cousin—unless of course, someone doesn't want someone else to know about a dark, hidden secret? Let's take a look at some secrets in my family.

## Grandfather: A Prophet

My father's mother was part of the Pentecostal Holiness movement, and his father (my grandfather) was a prophet in the Holiness movement.

Many people told me that my grandfather wasn't well-liked and that others wanted to run him off because he was so strongly opinionated, even in parts of the Holiness movement. Apparently, if you were going to be around him long you were going to live holy, and in the way, *he* interpreted holiness.

(Before we go any further, I want to be clear that I don't believe everyone who goes around claiming to be a prophet really is a prophet, but I had good reason to believe my grandfather was a prophet.)

My grandfather died when my dad was eleven, which is very significant to this story because at that stage in my father's life, my dad started to backslide and went far away from God. I really feel, looking back, that some of the decisions that occurred in that time opened some doors in my family. Over the years, we have had to place this stuff under the blood of Christ.

## Carrying a Mantle with Racism

My grandfather was a prophet, and later on in life God called me to be a prophet too. However, I had to trace our bloodline and go back in our past to heal some stuff that my grandfather had carried. My grandfather was a *racist*. God sees and knows our past, and He doesn't want any of His people overlooked or passed by because of color.

God had to reveal the sin of racism in my bloodline, something that God despised then and now. The Lord actually told me, "If you want to walk in your grandfather's mantle, it must be cleansed." So I started investigating my grandfather's history. I quickly discovered what needed to be cleansed. My grandfather was a prophet *and a member of the Ku Klux Klan!* That's where racism entered into our bloodline. You mean, Charlie, that you were once a racist too? Yes, I was. I hated black or brown people because of the color of their skin. This had to be eradicated from my life and my bloodline; and today, I don't hate people at all. I am not a racist because I have placed that hatred under the blood of Christ.

> How much more, then, will the blood of Christ, who
> through the eternal Spirit offered himself unblemished to
> God, cleanse our consciences from acts that lead to death,
> so that we may serve the living God! (Hebrews 9:14)

In the Old Testament, the animal sacrifices were passive; the animals were victims because they didn't willingly give their lives to die for the sins of Israel. But Christ wasn't a passive victim. He *willingly* gave Himself as a sacrifice to cover all sin. Christ's blood is superior because it is perfect. Because Christ willingly offered Himself as a perfect sacrifice, our sins and our consciences, marred by evil works, have been cleansed. Sometimes, something is so serious that it has to be dealt with before we can move forward. For me, this problem was racism. God doesn't want this thread in any heart, including yours or mine.

## What Does Racism Have to Do with Rape and Restoration?

Both racism and rape hold the same weight when it comes to spiritual perversion. They both completely destroy and kill.

Our thinking is oftentimes in the moment. For example, we think about what we are eating for dinner or whether we should take the dogs out or leave it for our spouse when they come home, along with a multitude of other thoughts. This is how our minds work, and that is okay because this is how God made us. He expects us to use our brains and learn to handle the different responsibilities in life.

God's thinking isn't exactly this way. He isn't thinking about what you're going to eat tomorrow; that has already been provided for, whether you see it or not (Matthew 6:25). God's thinking is more generational in nature. He is thinking more along the lines of: "What can this person do to bring My glory to the next generation?" For this reason, I believe that we have to allow God to go back into our past history and clean it up to stop any further damage from continuing into the next generation. Once these sins are dealt with, it breaks the hold off of the future bloodlines of our families. This has to happen in order for generational blessings to go deeper in our lives.

*There are generational curses (like racism) and generational blessings (like hospitality).*

Have you ever noticed that some people are three or four generations into drugs and alcohol? Or that some people are three or four generations into welfare? Why is that? I can't speak for everyone, but some of this stuff are generational curses on their bloodline, and these curses have to be broken.

## The Messy Dog in My Rental House

Two years after my encounter with Jesus I was serving God and driving back to Vero Beach to work on one of my rental houses. On the drive I was listening to a teaching tape on generational curses, and that's when God spoke to me about generational blessings and told me I could clean the mantle of my grandfather. God started comparing my grandfather's mantel with this rental house that I had to clean up. My tenant had this old dog that left a disaster in the garage. The urine smell was so bad that I had to pressure wash the floors with bleach because that nasty dog had peed all over the garage. I had to remove up to about three feet of drywall all over the house and treat the floor with a two part epoxy paint that would seal the concrete just to keep the smell out. The dog went to the bathroom inside. Worse yet, it was like the dog just walked around and peed all over the floor and along the walls in the garage. It really was horrible, so I wasn't in the best of moods.

As I was driving I remembered about halfway through the series the Holy Spirit said to me, "Do you believe in generational curses?" I said, "Well, yeah! I'm listening to the teaching." Then the Holy Spirit said, "Do you believe in generational blessings?" Of course I said I did. He then said something very powerful to me that I would like to share with you now. I believe this is really going to help some of you overcome some serious things that you have had to deal with in your life.

The Holy Spirit said, "If you're willing to deal with a generational curse from your family line, then I'll show you a blessing that is an inheritance that you can recover." What He showed me next concerning bloodlines, authority, and cleansing was amazing.

He reminded me that I was a prophet through my grandfather's mantle of being a prophet. He showed me how I had to go back and clean his mantle because it was stained with racism.

Why was this important? Because racism, through my grandfather, had a *legal right to be in my bloodline*: it had a right to attack and work in me because my grandfather *had agreed* to it. Not only was he a prophet but also a member of the Ku Klux Klan! The whole weekend I was there, working on that dirty house, was really all about me receiving this prophetic mantle and learning how to walk in it.

## The Messy House is YOUR Fault!

The nasty dog didn't help the situation; in fact, that was what made it worse. While I was standing on the concrete floor working in that garage, God showed up. A physical, actually visual, glory cloud came in there where I was and He said to me, "The mess in this house is your fault! You're the owner of this house and you had a contract with your tenant that read 'No dogs'! You allowed her to keep a dog and opened up a legal right for this filth to come into your house." Sometimes we think it is God's fault or someone else's when, in fact, it is ours. Sometimes what we are dealing with actually has a right to be there *because we allowed it*. In the kingdom what you tolerate will dominate.

## My Grandfather's Grave Was Close By

After I cleaned my messy dog rental and while I was still in Vero Beach, I decided to go find a place to pray. I stopped off at a church called New Hope Ministries on 71st Avenue. Because it was a holiday weekend there were no cars in the parking lot, but it just so happened that the secretary was there that Monday, and she let me into the sanctuary to pray. I had an encounter with God that day. The Holy Spirit said to me, "I have given you the ability to see into the realm of the kingdom and I have shown you how to recover your spiritual inheritance."

After the encounter in the sanctuary, I left the building and, as I walked to my car, looked over the fence. On the side of the church property, there was a cemetery. About 500 feet from me was my grandfather's grave. I went to an opening at the end of the fence and found my grandfather's grave. That's when God began to speak to me about the revelation on true spiritual inheritance. Remember Abraham, Isaac, and Jacob? (See Acts 7:3, 8.) What is being passed down from our forefathers is being passed down to our children. This is when God told me about being in a covenant with God. This is why we have to deal with abuse. We have to get it out of our bloodlines and our paths. We have to cover our future generations from this type of tragedy.

## How Does This Apply to the Church?

I had personally allowed that rental house of mine to get messy. Because my tenant was faithfully paying the rent, I looked the other way. I knew she had that dog, and I did nothing about it. The Lord told me that preachers are no different. As long as people are paying their tithes, the preachers are willing to look the other way and overlook their sin. The preachers were not addressing it: and that's why there was such a mess within the house of God. True cleaning must start on the inside of the house first. This is why God was redeeming His church, the bride of Christ. God said to me, "If you're going to be a prophet for Me, you will not be allowed to overlook the contract of My Word."

## Redemption Is Individual and Corporate

> He redeemed us in order that the blessing given to Abraham might come to the Gentiles through Christ Jesus, so that by faith we might receive the promise of the Spirit. (Galatians 3:14)

Man or woman of God, in order to become what God has called you to be, you must first be willing to go back and fix things that were already broken in the beginning. As a pastor, I have had to fix a lot of stuff that I didn't break right there in my own community. When God sees that you are willing to take responsibility for something that you didn't do, and that you will go ahead and fix it to allow the people around you to heal, then that is when you will start walking in true spiritual authority. God, as good as He is, wants us (men and women alike) to walk in true Spirit-led authority. This is our real divine inheritance.

Too many of our churches are working in "forced submission" *without intimacy* because we are being groomed to walk that way. God has to clean this out of our lives and our churches. This means that we, His church, have to be healed and put back together. This is what I will cover in the next several chapters, but let's talk about the bad stuff first.

# Chapter 3: The Day That Shattered My Life

E arlier I shared a story about a fifteen-year-old girl who was attending her own prom and was brutally raped. There are many parts to this story that are extremely sad, but to me one of the really tragic parts is the fact that there were many people there. This happened in a public place! One report said that people witnessed the attack outside and on the school grounds, yet they just walked by and paid no attention to her cries for help. The administrators and security were all inside, at the event, while she was being viciously attacked outside. The report also said the girl looked as if she had been treated as less than human. This all occurred at a location that should have been a safe place for all kids—her high school.

## One Tragic Day

In one day, that girl's life changed forever. My life, too, was destroyed in one day. On that day, my life changed forever. Over the years, I have credited God for bringing me back to normalcy.

Statistically, one out of every thirty-three American men has been the victim of an attempted or completed rape in their lifetime.[5]

As I mentioned before, my parents were always active and involved with the church: my dad was a deacon. Another deacon family in the

---

5. "Scope of the Problem: Statistics," RAINN, accessed May 02, 2019, https://www.rainn.org/statistics/scope-problem.

church was close friends with my parents. At that time in my life I didn't have any reason to believe there was anything seriously wrong in the other family. For the sake of their identity in this story, I am going to call my attacker "Stephen."

It was around 1966 or 1967, and I was seven years old at the time. One day I went to Stephen's house, just like normal, because both of my parents had things to do; and so Stephen's mom was watching me. His mom had to go to the store and left me with him at their house. He was seventeen years old. We were sitting on the couch in the den. (Homes had dens back then, not TV or entertainment rooms.) At first I felt no reason to be afraid or fearful. Nothing was abnormal.

While Stephen's mom was at the store and gone for a while, he came over to me and started physically touching me (molesting me). Then he pulled out a knife and put it to my throat; and at seven years of age, he brutally sodomized (raped) me. It was the worst experience of my life and it was a time that I have never forgotten.

## Never to Be Forgotten

One online article dealing with home invasions and robberies suggests that when a person's home is robbed, it is as if a part of the owner's physical life has been attacked as well.[6] Our home is supposed to be the safest place on earth. The article goes on to suggest that when someone's home is compromised, it can cause things like anger, sleeplessness for months and sometimes years. Some people who have had their homes broken into actually can go for most of their lives being a light sleeper. This alone can cause an immense amount of pressure and stress on the person's body over time. This article referred only to home robberies. Can you imagine how much worse it is for someone who was raped and physically attacked? If this much damage can be caused by a home invasion, how much more damage is there for the victim of rape?

---

6. Julie Bawden Davis, "Burglary Can Leave Emotional Scars: Anger, Fear May Be More Damaging Than Material Loss," *Los Angeles Times*, January 2, 1994, accessed May 02, 2019, http://articles.latimes.com/1994-01-02/realestate/re-7835_1_emotional-damage.

How long will it be until that person ever really gets a good night's sleep again? Or will they ever?

If you have never been physically or sexually attacked, you might not ever understand the mind and emotions of a person who has. People who have been brutally raped or sexually assaulted are sometimes altered and marred for life; they never mentally or emotionally heal from it. Even years after the attack some people, especially women or young children, build really high "security walls" or defense mechanisms and do not allow many people to cross their lines. Some people who have dealt with this kind of trauma may constantly be on high alert and paying close attention to the surroundings. They may ask a lot of questions that you may feel are unnecessary or make someone feel awkward around them. And, if something doesn't feel right to them in anyway, they will normally be the first to call someone or a situation out. This condition is called *hypervigilance.*

In some cases, you, the person who has nothing to do with the victim's attack, may even be singled out for no apparent reason. When a person is attacked, whether their mind chooses to suppress that moment or not, there can be certain times when a person can remember a certain building, room, couch or bed, a smell, a culture, or even a person's cologne or clothing. Sometimes it's the personality of their attacker that, when encountered in someone else, can quickly trigger the pain again. This is why those affected in this way may not "like" others that remind them of their attacker—even though that person did nothing at all. Sometimes the person who that rape victim doesn't like is *you!* You may have certain traits that remind them of their attacker. Being a pastor, I am constantly reminding myself that we really don't know why a person acts a certain way. For this reason, we must learn not to prejudge someone we really don't know or understand. I think it is best most of the time to just leave it alone until God deals with it.

### Tell It Loud and Clear!

One statistic suggests that out of 1,000 rapes, 995 attackers will go free. And only 230 are actually reported to the police. Of the 230 reported to the police, only *five* individual attackers will receive a felony conviction.[7]

Some people hide the fact that they were raped or attacked. I understand because it is one of the most humiliating events in your life. If this is you, I am not attempting to diminish you if you never told another person. I understand why.

One statistic suggests that only one out of every four sexual assaults is reported at all.[8] Whether you decided to tell someone or not doesn't matter right now. Back then, at the time, I knew I had to tell someone. That same day, when Stephen's mom came home from the store, I told her. Sometime after, and still the same day as well, I also told his dad what happened. They assured me that they would talk to my parents about it; and at seven years of age, I believed them. The fact is that Stephen's parents *never told my parents* at all.

For at least the rest of that year's summer, I went over there to his house from time to time, but I also became aggressive. I made sure I was never alone with him again; and if I had to be, I made sure I was in a situation where I could get out of there if needed. I don't recall him ever trying to do something like that to me again after that one single time.

## Tragedy Can Happen Anytime

Keep in mind, we were both from the same church—his parents and my parents were on the church board together and extremely close friends. This seventeen-year-old boy had serious problems. Once Stephen was at the back of the church and actually took a knife and carved up the pews. This young man had something about knives! Stephen, as I have been calling him, was evil; he was a bad boy sitting right there in the church. To be honest, I really don't know much about him, but doesn't this type of behavior make you wonder how he ever got that far? Something must have happened to him! Something had to have

---

7. "The Criminal Justice System: Statistics," RAINN, accessed May 02, 2019, https://www.rainn.org/statistics/criminal-justice-system.

8. Ibid.

changed the course of his life to turn him into such an evil person. I'm sure he wasn't born that way.

## God Heals Every Pain

> The Lord is close to the brokenhearted and saves those
> who are crushed in spirit. (Psalm 34:18)

Reading my story may bring back some really painful memories for some. Odds are, either you or someone you know has been raped. Or maybe you were the one abusing someone else? Regardless, you are probably dealing with some painful memories right now. If this story has brought your pain to the surface for the first time or made it reappear after a long time, don't ignore it. Don't suppress it. God has to bring to the surface what needs to be healed. Now is the time! If you have to pause and talk to the Lord, do it right now. If not, let's continue.

## How Does This Apply to the Church?

I was raped at a young age. I had a knife held to my throat, and I was viciously attacked! How do we connect my rape to the local church? Remember: *Forced intimacy without relationship is rape*. Every week good, innocent people walk through the doors of our churches, and some turn around and never return.

One 2017 report looked at 1,000 American Protestant evangelical churches in 2013 and 2016, and the findings were staggering: "65 percent of churches are declining or plateaued."[9]

Why? Church regulations, the privilege to remain committed to a local church, are growing while church relationships (kingdom building) are dying. Church regulations *without any relational involvement* is nothing more than taking advantage of good people. To be blunt, this type of abuse is very similar to rape: it is like taking something that is

---

9. "Dispelling the 80 Percent Myth of Declining Churches," Thom S. Rainer (blog), accessed May 29, 2009, https://thomrainer.com/2017/06/dispelling-80-percent-myth-declining-churches/.

extremely valuable to someone and using it for someone else's pleasure. Christ came to set us free. He didn't come to bind us up again through church rules and regulations.

Don't get me wrong—I believe in order, I believe in authority, and I believe in governing structures (Romans 13:1–2).

I speak as a pastor; and, regrettably, we have turned our churches into church growth campaigns, where numbers count more than anything else. Pastor or church leader, God didn't call you to build a church by the use of numbers—He called you to build a mature church, where people's needs are truly met. A real church body is a place where the sheep can get healed and sent out properly, in order to make an impact on the communities in which they live.

Likewise, we have created an environment in church leadership in which church services and attendance are becoming the criteria for the primary relationship with God. God's relationship is Monday through Sunday, not what we do or how we serve on a Sunday morning. Fact is, you can be in the church all the time and still never have a true transformation. Stephen, the seventeen-year-old man who raped me, was there in the church, carving up pews in the back with a knife. He grew up in a deacon's home and look how he turned out.

# Chapter 4: *Monster*–What I Had Become

H ave you ever been in a restaurant or public building and stopped long enough to look around and just wonder who else is in that area with you? I think if this happened, and we could look into the past and future of all of those individuals around us throughout the day, we might be shocked and surprised at the same time. The reality is that we may never know who might be sitting right next to us. Consider all the people you pass each day or sit with while at college or work, or who are nearby in a local restaurant.

The book *You Belong to Me and Other True Cases*, by Ann Rule, tells a story about a man named Phil Williams who went to elementary school, first grade to be exact, and sat right next to a boy by the name of Sylvan Bishop. According to Phil, Sylvan used to constantly turn to him and tell him things like, "One day I hope to be on the FBI's Most Wanted List." At the time, they were in first grade; and looking back, they were just kids. Phil was sure Sylvan didn't mean it. Or did he?

It was September 1970, and by then this young, innocent first-grader, Sylvan Bishop, was eighteen years old. According to Ann Rule's book:

> Sylvan Bishop reported that he had discovered two decomposed bodies in a woods west of Vero Beach. The victims were eventually identified as Kathleen Phillips, nineteen, and her friend, Joanna Malandrino, twenty. They hadn't been reported missing because their families thought they were on a trip from their home in Hollywood,

Florida, to see Joanne's grandmother up in New Jersey. They *had* traveled north on I-95, but they hadn't gone more than a hundred miles before they developed car trouble and stopped at a service station in Vero Beach in the wee hours of the morning of September 1.

Sylvan Bishop was the night attendant. Apparently working toward his life's ambition, Sylvan had already been to reform school in Okeechobee and Marianna, to jail in Appalachee, and in a state mental institution for six weeks. The naive girls from Hollywood, Florida, thought he was being exceptionally kind when he offered to drive them into town at the end of his shift, and they waited until he got off duty at 6:30 a.m.

No one ever saw them alive after that. Sylvan Bishop had indeed made the "big time" in crime, and he was charged with two counts of first-degree murder. When Philip Williams heard that, he recalled Sylvan's childhood goal and remembered the kid at the next desk in first grade. He realized then that killers weren't always strangers; a murderer could be someone who was so much a part of your own world that you might never suspect him—or her.[10]

This rapist and murderer, Sylvan D. Bishop, was born on September 23, 1951, and died on August 12, 2005, at the age of fifty-three. He died on death row for the two murders mentioned above and was buried in the Florida State Prison Cemetery in Raiford, Union County, Florida.[11]

Earlier I shared about the girl at her high school prom who was gang raped for roughly two hours; more than likely, you didn't know her and still don't. Same with me. I don't know anything about that young girl other than what was reported in the news. The same with this story

---

10. Ann Rule, *You Belong to Me and Other True Cases* (London: Warner, 1997).

11. "Sylvan D. Bishop," Findagrave.com, accessed May 02, 2019, https://www.finda-grave.com/memorial/113025804/sylvan-d-bishop.

about Sylvan Bishop. Who knows anything about him? Do you? Again, more than likely, you don't know anything about him other than what is being written right here. To be exact, if I were a betting man, I would suggest that you never, ever heard of Sylvan Bishop until you read his name for the first time in this chapter. Am I right? (I bet I am! ☺)

Me, on the other hand: I knew Sylvan Bishop. I knew this man, this rapist and cold-blooded murderer who killed those two innocent young women and then buried their bodies in the woods in Vero Beach, Florida. Sylvan Bishop was the seventeen-year-old who raped me at knifepoint when I was seven years old in his parents' home while I was on the couch. This is the "Stephen" of the previous chapter.

This story may not have hit home for you, but it does for me. I was seven; he was seventeen at the time. We both went to the same church! His parents were close friends with my parents! This was the person carving in the pews; and roughly one year later, he raped and murdered two women. Do you see the evil parallel between the two stories? He used a knife to rape me and a knife to kill both women. This man had a serious problem that destroyed many lives.

### Silence Isn't the Best Way

Looking back, this is probably one reason why his parents never had a chance to talk to mine about Sylvan raping me. Sylvan was in and out of rehabs, mental hospitals, and jail; and soon after, he raped and murdered two innocent ladies. I am not exactly sure if his parents even wanted to talk about it at all with mine, but maybe this is why they didn't say anything. Another reason why his parents might not have said anything to my parents may have been that shortly after this man attacked me at his home, our church went through a horrible situation with the pastor; and my dad, a deacon, and Sylvan's dad, also a deacon, were at odds with each other because of it. Or it just might have been because Sylvan's parents wanted to hide this under the rug in order to protect their son. I don't know why, but for me this caused some serious problems. It caused me to mistakenly believe that my dad wouldn't stand up for me for most of my life. I felt that if something happened between the church and me, my dad would be more than willing to throw me under the bus to save his or the church's reputation. This is what helped forge me into the monster I would later become.

## Growing Up at Seven

That day I was attacked by Sylvan, that little seven-year-old boy with the tender heart no longer had a tender heart. This attack triggered fear in me for the rest of my life. From that moment on, I made sure that nobody was ever going to do something like that to me again. I decided that day that I was never going to be manhandled again. That attack also caused me to have a fight-or-flight instinct from that time on. I realized back then that I could not trust my parents, his parents, or anyone for that matter.

At the time, I thought his parents had talked to my parents; and because my dad did nothing, I assumed my dad was a coward and would not help me because he did nothing about it to ever protect me or defend me. This opened up a lot of anger, hurt, and rejection in my life. I possessed a hidden rage, tucked deep down inside, waiting to go off like a time bomb one day.

I have heard it said that when a person has a bitter heart that is not healed, the Enemy has a legal right to torment and control that person. It's called bitter root judgment. In other words, you become what you hate. I truly believe that was the root issue of fear and control that led me to become the monster that date raped Susie on my eighteenth birthday. You become what you hate. To make matters worse, Susie had been a virgin, and she became pregnant from my abuse. We will discuss her story in greater detail later in this book.

## The Real Truth Will Eventually Come Out

I was thirty-five years old when my dad heard about how this man, Sylvan, sexually attacked me. He had tears in his eyes; he was shocked, and he was angry. The fact is, my father wasn't a coward at all. He was actually the man I wanted to believe he was as I was growing up. He truly was a man's man, just like I depicted him earlier in this book. He stood up for us and what was right. My accusations of my dad protecting the church and throwing me under the bus turned out to be untrue. It was the exact opposite. My dad knew nothing about any of it. I know now that if my dad would have found out about this attack on me when I was seven years old, he would have gone after that family. He would have dealt with it to make sure that it never happened again to me or anyone else.

## Monsters in Our Homes

One rape statistic state that "55% of rape attacks take place on or near the home."[12] Right there in Sylvan's home, just down on the other side of town, a place I once trusted, I was raped. At the time, my parents trusted that family. They had no idea that this man was a monster, a murderer in the making. If they had, they wouldn't have sent me over there to be watched by them. But look again at that statistic again. Fifty-five percent! I am one of those represented by that statistic, someone who was attacked near a home. How many reading this are also one of these victims? Many rape victims say that their attacker was either someone they knew and trusted or someone with whom they'd had some form of acquaintance at one time. It isn't just the random attack on a rape victim that happens; it often occurs with the person you actually knew and felt comfortable enough to put your guard down around.

## Monsters in Our Churches

An article on KSL.com from November 18, 2018, states that a woman was assaulted while playing the organ at a Centerville, Utah, church.[13] According to the article, the seventy-one-year-old woman was in the church alone, quietly playing the organ around 9:30 p.m.

---

12. "Scope of the Problem: Statistics," RAINN, accessed May 02, 2019, https://www.rainn.org/statistics/scope-problem.

13. Jacob Klopfenstein, "Woman Assaulted While Playing Organ at Centerville Church," *KSL*, November 18, 2018, accessed May 02, 2019, https://www.ksl.com/article/46429945/woman-assaulted-while-playing-organ-at-centerville-church.

or so. The building was locked down and she was alone, or so she thought. According to the report, it isn't clear why the attacker entered the building, and there were no weapons involved. The woman stated that she heard some pounding on the chapel door of the church that continued for several minutes. The police report stated that the attacker threw something through the window on the east side of the church. About thirty minutes later, more than likely, the attacker got into the chapel through another way and started choking her. It was not reported that the person who pounded on the door was the same person that got into the chapel later to choke her.

She wasn't sexually attacked, but she suffered minor bruises on her neck. She ended up passing out during the attack, so she wasn't able to get a good look at the person's face. This isn't a story about rape, but it is a story about assault of the worst kind: to an elderly woman alone in the church. The church should be a place where she felt safe and secure. Now, she would be haunted with this the rest of her life. Thank God nothing worse happened to her that night.

## How Does This Apply to the Church?

One statistic suggests that 15 percent of rapes take place on public property.[14] When we read something like this, we might think of the fifteen-year-old rape victim at the high school prom that we talked about earlier in the book. Or maybe it was at a mall in the late evening when it was dark and the lady didn't get to her car safely; instead, she was attacked and placed in another vehicle. Sometimes it is inside buildings, like at a workplace or when leaving work to go home. Most, however, don't assume that this 15 percent would include a church, but it can. Why?

Tragedy can happen at any time and in any place. Unfortunately, another type of tragedy is happening all across our country every weekend in our churches. People are coming in and out of our churches

---

14. "Scope of the Problem: Statistics," RAINN, accessed May 02, 2019, https://www.rainn.org/statistics/scope-problem.

every week; and instead of them being transformed into Christ's likeness, they are leaving—oftentimes unchanged. This is *not* how it is supposed to be. The church doesn't exist to build itself; it exists to build (and equip) the people within it. When we attempt to change a person's life through regulations, without relationship, in a sense we are producing *servants* and *not sons and daughters* of God.

In the same way, when we try to force a covenant relationship with someone without spiritual intimacy, then in reality we are doing no less than raping them. Rape is when someone is forced without consent. Spiritual rape is when we place our regulations on someone, making them convert, in order to maintain a relationship with them. In other words, if we force them to line up like we want them to and do what we want them to do and serve how we want them to—then and only then can they be in a church-based relationship with us. However, if someone comes along who might not fit that mold, we church leaders are too quick to *blacklist* them, or cut them out of the fold, because we are scared that they might cause trouble or try to steal our sheep away. Have you ever wondered why some people that you don't understand showed up at the church in the first place? Just maybe, God wants to do something different in your church this time. Perhaps He wants to lead us into covenant relationship with Him and each other—instead of forced intimacy, which never works.

# Chapter 5: *Broken*—What I Created

Relationships are vitally important. Over the years, the divine appointments God has given me personally are memories that I will hold on to for the rest of my life. Some of them are right here in this book. Not all of God's divine intervention are special visits, like when He met with me that day in the garage. (You know, the day that He talked to me about my grandfather's mantle in Chapter 2.) Many times, God decides to work His miracles through other people. There have been various times when I seriously needed a divine miracle, a supernatural breakthrough, and it didn't come through a dust cloud, an angel, or a supernatural visitation from God—it came through people just like you and me. It came through people who heard from the Lord for me! In many cases, they were people from whom I least expected to receive a miracle.

It has been said that whenever God is getting ready to do something new, you can rest assured that God will bring some new relationships into your life. It is through those new relationships that, more than likely, God will choose to work in order to take you where you wouldn't have been able to go on your own. Sometimes this isn't the case though. Occasionally, God has to *remove* old friends out of your life in order to get you to focus on Him more. The reason is that some of the old friends just might be the ones who are causing a lot of problems; and whether you see it or not, God does. So God does whatever is needed.

Do you remember David and Jonathan in the Bible?

> Jonathan said to David, "Go in peace, for we have sworn friendship with each other in the name of the Lord, saying, 'The Lord is witness between you and me, and between your descendants and my descendants forever.'" Then David left, and Jonathan went back to the town. (1 Samuel 20:42)

They had a pure relationship with each other—one in which they were both willing to put their lives on the line in order to give their best to each other. This is a perfect example of a best friend in life, or someone who truly sticks closer than a brother (Proverbs 18:24). This is what love, laughter, and living is supposed to look like. It isn't superficial. It is real. The power of love, working through a person's life, gives them the ability to choose to serve and love another at all costs.

Being in ministry and a pastor now for a long time, I have come across many couples who truly loved each other at one time. Without a doubt, they were passionate for the Lord and each other, and they both heard God and knew that they were supposed to marry each other. But something happened along the way; sometimes it's very obvious. The man or woman cheats on the other, and horrible things are done inside the privacy of their home. Maybe it wasn't anything to do with what they did; maybe it was because one of them lost their job or, worse yet, a child.

Sometimes it's that one of them or a family member goes through a really dreadful prolonged sickness, and when they come out of it, the experience has sapped all of their time, money, and resources and just left them with nothing. I can go on and on with story after story that I have witnessed firsthand with people that I have met. Regardless of the "how," the reality is that now there is a precious couple that no longer wants to be together. My wife and I have had counseling sessions with other couples in our church, and some who were outside of our church, and in ministry in which the fire—the love for each other—just went stone cold. This is a sad thing to see, and it is a bad situation to be in.

One statistic on pregnancies states: "About 4 out of 10 children were born to unwed mothers. Nearly two-thirds were born to mothers under the age of 30."[15] Did you catch that? Nearly half of our children born today are to unwed mothers. First of all, this isn't good for the child. God's orchestration is for both parents to raise their kids, not one. Secondly, this puts an unnecessary burden on the mother because she has to do it all herself. I know that some of you reading this are currently in these shoes right now; or maybe you grew up without a mom or a dad in the home. There is a void sometimes when this happens. In my case, and because of me, Susie was now facing life with a child as a single mom.

## Susie and the Engagement

Not surprisingly, Susie and I were no longer friends. We were no longer passionate about each other and the thought of a true friendship relationship, like the one we see in Jonathan and David, wasn't even on the horizon.

Susie and I went to the same church; she was a huge part of the youth group. We both liked each other, but she had a huge crush on me. We'd go out with the youth and have dinner after church on a Sunday night. She was a few days from her sixteenth birthday, and it was my eighteenth birthday that fatal night when I raped her. During this same time, I was engaged to be married to somebody else. I mean … talk about a scumbag! *I* was *the scumbag*! (If you don't hate me through some of this book, then you aren't really reading it!) Seriously, I got one girl pregnant *by force* at a time when I was engaged to another woman, and now I was running from it all. I was denying that the baby was mine and trying to make my engagement work, but God had other plans.

## The Other Woman

I got engaged when I was eighteen, the same time that I got Susie pregnant. Obviously, I was denying that fact to the woman to whom I

---

15. "Single Mother Statistics," *Single Mother Guide*, April 08, 2019, accessed May 02, 2019, https://singlemotherguide.com/single-mother-statistics/.

was engaged. Let's discuss that for a moment. How would you feel if you were engaged to be married to someone and someone else was going around saying that this person, the man that you were about to marry, got someone else pregnant? Keep in mind that Susie wasn't outspoken about the fact that I got her pregnant. Truth be told, she wasn't telling anyone; however, some people found out and the gossip spread. There were those talking way more than Susie or me.

However, my fiancée was also a victim because of what I put her through. I was lying to her and to others. I was telling people that the baby wasn't mine, that I had nothing to do with Susie's dilemma. My actions, my sin, was not only hurting Susie, it was hurting my fiancée too. In fact, it was hurting many other people. I was the bad boy in the youth group. The pastor told my dad that he wasn't qualified to be a deacon anymore because of the lifestyle of his kid—*me*! Charlie!

This is why our actions and our decisions in life are so important. Everything we do affects someone else. Sometimes, I think that we create holes from which only God can rescue us. In this case, I had created not just a hole, but a crater—a pit too deep for anyone to get out of! If it were not for God's grace and mercy, looking beyond my stupid, selfish decisions then, I would probably be dead. This stuff will eventually catch up to you. Someone will eventually say that they have had enough and that they will eventually snap. This was the case here.

Keep in mind that this was several decades ago; this wasn't in the twenty-first century, when some might think this is what true fathering looks like now. (It isn't, by the way. Real men will stick with their wives and children for life—until God separates them at death. Real men will be honest and hardworking, providing for and protecting their family.) That wasn't me back then. To be honest, I was a *real* jerk! I don't know how to paint that picture within one small chapter, but I hope you get the understanding of just how much I was forgiven when Christ forgave me.

> "But I want you to know that the Son of Man has authority on earth to forgive sins." (Mark 2:10)

54

Susie was the innocent one. Whatever you get from this book, make sure that you get that. Her story illustrates a deep love for someone and the ability to forgive a person at a level that is uncommon to many. I believe that in Susie's heart, she forgave me when I attacked her, got her pregnant, and then ran from all of it while trying to make an engagement happen that didn't work. Prior to all of this, she was a good little girl. Back then I called her "Sweet Susie" because she was so kind, loving, and sweet. She was innocent and she cared—you could tell that from the first time you met her. That was who she was until she met me, the idiot who almost ruined her life. I did not realize how sweet and forgiving Susie really was until much later, when Jesus walked through the wall and opened my eyes and introduced me to Mr. Love Himself. Until that encounter, I did not understand love or how true love changed hearts. Sadly, it was over sixteen years after the attack (that's two years of denial and fourteen years of marriage) before I had this life-changing encounter with Jesus.

I was not there for my son's birth, so Susie had the baby on her own, and eventually I went back to her and we got married. By that time, we were both out of high school, and life was moving along. The worst was behind us, so we thought. Susie walked in continual forgiveness toward me, trying the best that she could to be a mom at such a young age, and toughed it out. Even when Susie couldn't deal with me, she still tried.

## Learning to Live with Each Other

After a while, I became successful in Vero Beach. We were in our ninth year of marriage. The first two or three years were pretty good: working, living life, serving God, and going to church. I heard a preacher from Texas talking about the sin of pornography and alcohol. He was talking about how sin is like a fence made out of barbed wire. I felt like he was talking directly to me because he was addressing how Christians must get off the fence. He said that he didn't know about Florida, but in Texas the fences were made out of barbed wire. Even though I was convicted at that point, I rejected the Lord's voice and did not repent; and believe me, I needed to get off that fence. It was that week that I took a turn for the worse and walked away from God. The pornography and alcohol addiction moved in fast and got me. I had become a heathen of the worst kind, and I quickly found myself in a broken and backslidden condition.

In the meantime, Susie was trying to make it all work and carrying way too much responsibility. I was hooked on pornography, spending money like crazy, and basically losing control: literally all forms of self-control. I was completely backslidden and way deeper into sin at this time than I had been when I got Susie pregnant in high school.

We all miss it sometimes in life. Sometimes our spouse wakes up one morning and they are fine, and the next day it's like they fell off of the deep end. This normally occurs because something bad had just happened; some bad news had just come in. This happens a lot today. Between family, work, church, and all kinds of other responsibilities, it is easy to get to the end of the day and have nothing left to offer. Many couples walk in this daily. So, sometimes, we just snap. As I mentioned earlier, it was at this time, in our ninth year of marriage, that I backslid so horribly and just completely snapped. I turned into a worse monster than ever before. I went over the edge into deep pornography again. Susie knew it was wrong. She knew I was doing all of the stuff I knew not to do, and she was done. How could I blame her?

## Corruption Creates Corruption

I had become very perverted and corrupt, so I taught Susie how to go to the bars with me. The monster I was and the one Susie once knew was now living again—in her home. She became the person with me at the bars this time, but sometimes it wasn't with me; sometimes we were with other people. Before long, I no longer trusted her and she no longer trusted me. But I pushed her past her limits.

*Business Insider* came up with nine reasons people often snap. I want to share some of the top reasons:

One was that the person was being placed in a life-or-death situation.

Another one was over family matters.

One was due to the environment that they were in.[16]

I pushed Susie too far. I went right back to who I had been in high school—deep sin, the thing Susie didn't want to be connected with then or now. And when I went back to that, I really went back and I took Susie with me. Susie had now become what I was: broken. I created a broken vessel in the person that I had grown to love. She was broken because I was a monster again!

> "Then it goes and takes with it seven other spirits more wicked than itself, and they go in and live there. And the final condition of that person is worse than the first. That is how it will be with this wicked generation." (Matthew 12:45)

## When God Used an Atheist

Things were falling apart in our marriage. Neither of us were being honest or faithful at all during this time. I was blowing through all kinds of vices. One day, an atheist businessman took me to lunch and told me, "Listen, you know, I'm an atheist, but you're about to lose your marriage. And you're going to lose your business, too, if you're not careful. You might want to go find Jesus."

This wasn't from a pastor or a close friend. This was coming from an atheist, a person who didn't even believe in God! I was that messed up! It's one thing when someone in the church has to tell you to wake up; it's another issue altogether when God has to use someone that doesn't believe in Him to get your life back in order. For me, this was a turning point. This was when God began to bring the good seed up in my life, that which was real in me—His heart

---

16. Rebecca Harrington, "The 9 Reasons Why People Snap, According to a Neurobiologist," *Business Insider*, April 27, 2016, accessed May 02, 2019, https://www.businessinsider.com/why-people-snap-2016-4#2-insult-2.

and kingdom. It was a long process, but I began to change. In time, Susie began to see it as well.

## Restoration Can Happen

I have personally watched God restore my life. Truth be told, if God wasn't a loving and forgiving God, He should have killed me. Or, at the least, I should have ended up in jail or received some type of serious punishment. I have watched God restore our marriage, my business, and our finances. Last but not least, I have watched God restore my call to speak and minister the gospel to others. All this time, God had been watching me—Charlie. God saw who I would become one day, not just who I was back then. This is how God sees you too.

> "For I know the plans I have for you," declares the Lord,
> "plans to prosper you and not to harm you, plans to give
> you hope and a future." (Jeremiah 29:11)

Maybe your life, business, marriage, or family is in a total mess right now. Maybe you are that monster; or, even worse, maybe you created a monster and that person now causing you harm is an image of what you once were. This is something that only God can fix. Giving this all over to Him is what you have to do. It is easy to give it to Him initially but tough to carry out day by day. Give your life over to God; give your mess over to Him. Don't worry about the outcome; let Him seamlessly seal everything back up again. He did it with our marriage and family and my life, and I know that God can restore yours.

## Stick It Out

In fact, it is believed that those who get married, then divorced, and then marry the same person again end up living a much better life together long-term compared to those who get married, divorce, and move on to marry someone different. One blog post says this about marrying the same person again:

"Statistics for restored marriages, where ex-spouses remarry each other, may be somewhat surprising. While statistics in *Psychology Today* suggest that 67% of second marriages and 73% of third marriages end in divorce, things seem to go a little better for people who remarry their spouses...72% of reunited partners stayed together"[17]

> Restore to me the joy of your salvation and grant me a willing spirit, to sustain me. (Psalm 51:12)

She snapped! Susie snapped because I drove her to it! I have said this before: I never needed a map to get to "Stupid-ville." I knew exactly where that town was. (I still do, for that matter!) Why did she snap? Because I was further gone than ever before. I went back to deep sin, and I had promised to never do that again. Pornography, adultery, heavy drinking, and spending cash like it grew on a tree somewhere will catch up to you and eventually destroy you. She watched it happen right in front her, but this time it pushed her over the edge. She couldn't go back to the time in her life when she was sixteen and I was eighteen, and she was pregnant. Things had changed for her now. Susie got to a place where she didn't care to be redeemed anymore. She didn't care to even have me as a husband, regardless of how hard I tried after I finally began to straighten up and clean up my life again. She was broken and there wasn't anything left. It was so bad at our home that she would flat-out tell me to my face that she didn't want God to restore our marriage. This was painful at the time. Really painful!

> Since you call on a Father who judges each person's work impartially, live out your time as foreigners here in reverent fear. For you know that it was not with perishable things such as silver or gold that you were redeemed from the empty way of life handed down to you from your ancestors, but with the precious blood of Christ, a lamb without blemish or defect. (1 Peter 1:17–19)

---

17. Audrey M. Jones, "Restore Marriage After Divorce," *LoveToKnow*, accessed May 02, 2019, https://divorce.lovetoknow.com/Restore_Marriage_After_Divorce.

## How Does This Apply to the Church?

Every now and then, the church is in a state in which it doesn't want to be redeemed either. I believe the American church is there now. We have spent so much of our time and resources learning to "do church" and have church "our way" that I am not so sure that God's hand is resting on some of the stuff that we have been calling "church" anymore.

God is trying to bring us back to Him. To *Him*! Not the pews, the music, the great speaking skills that pastors work so hard to attain, the programs, or the service for Him. All of that is great, but the greater promise is when we exist *for* Him. Oftentimes, we are working far more for something else than we are for our Creator, Jesus Christ. He wants us back. He wants to redeem us. He wants to pour His Spirit on our lives in a way that we have never seen or experienced before. He wants to turn our hearts back to spending time with Him—with living and dwelling in His presence as our highest priority. When we do this, when we choose to live like this and not like the heathen, everything will change. This is when our church services will be transformed from a two-hour "happy hour with people who love Jesus" to a true habitation time with the Creator—a moment in time when God visits us in divine power and revelation. This is what the church needs right now. This is when we, pastors and leaders, must turn and turn fast. God wants to redeem His church, His bride, and we have to let Him do it. Too many people get saved *to the church* and *not to Jesus Christ*. I am not against commitment to a local church. Remember, I am a pastor, so I see the importance of commitment, but our commitment must be to Jesus first and foremost, not to an organization.

# Chapter 6: Hurt People Hurt People

Hatred stirs up conflict, but love covers over all wrongs.
(Proverbs 10:12)

Have you ever noticed that hurt people hurt each other? This often happens because the hurt person is carrying unresolved forgiveness toward someone else in their life. When we carry unforgiveness, resentment, and hatred toward others, it becomes a festering cancer inside your heart; and though you might not see it, it is there. Even if you do not feel any side effects of it right now, eventually it will come to the surface and destroy you if it goes untreated. How do we get the cancer of unforgiveness out?

Before we answer this, I want to go back to my story. I just completely lost it, and I knew better. I had a business partner in the lighting business. I was rolling in thousands of dollars a week of just play money and still taking care of the household needs. Let's face it: the cash was rolling in like waves on the Florida shore. My business partner thought I was crazy at the time. I think we both were. Money wasn't an issue at all, but my pornography habit was way too deep, and I knew better. I was doing everything imaginable and so was Susie. Finally, Susie asked for a divorce. She had had it. She didn't care what it took. She didn't want me to go back to all the evil I had once done, but I had gone back; and believe me, it was much worse the second time around. Never return to bondage to something from which you were once set free.

It was during this time when God's conviction began to rest on me again. The Lord began to deal with me about how I was wrongfully spending the company money. I did not really want to be honest with my business partner at the time. I didn't know how God was going to work it out, but I knew He was leading me to change the way I handled money. God told me that if I couldn't be trusted with money now, He wouldn't trust me with money in the future. During this time, my wife had a conversation with my partner, and God worked it out through His intervention. It happened in such a way that it had to be only God. Susie made one statement about wanting what was fair in the divorce, and she know about all the under-the-table money we were taking. Because of that statement, my partner demanded that we go completely legit.

## The Power of Your Mother

I was at work in my lighting store one day and, unexpectedly, my mother walked directly into my office. Standing there, she told me that she wanted to talk to my checkbook. She said, "Charlie, every day of your life from when I knew I was pregnant I knew that there was a call of God on your life." I was stunned and watched her look at me. She then said, "I've prayed blessings upon your life until this day. Today I did not pray a blessing. Instead, I pronounced judgment on you and your checkbook. I'm telling you right now. You're about to go into a famine because you are addicted to pornography and in adulterous relationships. You have a calling of God on your life to be a prophet to the nations and instead you're in sin. You're not worthy to be accepted. You're not worthy to be a father in this condition." Then she prayed right there in front of me: "Today I judge you." She looked at me and said, "I gave the Holy Spirit permission to kill you if necessary because I *will* see you in heaven. You can come the easy way or the hard way. That's all up to you!"

With that, she walked out while I sat there, stunned. I knew Mom knew God, but she had never cursed or judged anybody—ever—to my knowledge. While still sitting there like I had just seen a ghost, she walked back in and said, "I don't know if you know this or not, but I love Jesus more than I love you." Then she walked back out the door.

This got my attention. Before this occurrence with my mother, I had everything. I was making enough money to take care of the house and plenty of money. I was foolish and arrogant too—because everything I touched turned to gold. I had enough money to pay all the bills, and I was hiding $3,000–$4,000 in my golf bag so I could live the party lifestyle with ease. I wasn't just playing golf. Instead I was buying hookers. I was going to parties and going marlin fishing in Costa Rica. I had no worries and all the cash I wanted. Pride will give you a false perspective of success.

It was at that moment—when Mom spoke—that everything I touched started falling apart. I lost the Midas touch. Suddenly, my businesses were going down the tubes because she had judged me with her authority as my mother, and the favor of God came off my life.

Until we have had a real heart-to-heart transformation with God, we are still the same person we were decades ago—the same one we often don't want to be. That was how it was for me. I still carried the DNA and the capability of doing the things God didn't want me involved in. Until my sexual sins and pornography were dealt with at a heart-to-heart level between me and God, they weren't going to go away. God has to go into our lives and gut them and heal them; we have to make sure that sin never comes back. This requires us to change the course of our lives and change the patterns that we once lived by.

## Addictions Are Addictions until God Removes Them

Take a gambling addict. I don't know if you were one or ever met one, but once a person is deeply involved in this vice, the habit is as addictive as crack cocaine or heroin. We all know the stories of how someone lost everything through gambling. How does it happen? It is an addiction to a sin that can't be broken—except through the Lord. Gambling is powerful, and it can destroy your life. I was a gambler with my life, but not with slot machines. I may not have gone to casinos, but I did, many times, just do really stupid stuff with our hard-earned money. Sometimes it isn't gambling that can bring your life's work down to the pit; sometimes it is overspending money on things you don't really need but you buy anyway.

For those of you who struggle with gambling or know someone that does, here are a few sobering statistics on the power and grip of a gambling addiction: "Over 80 percent of American adults gamble on a yearly basis. Three to five gamblers out of every hundred struggles with a gambling problem. As many as 750,000 young people, ages 14 to 21 has a gambling addiction."[18] Those numbers are astoundingly large!

## Sin Itself Is Addictive

Gambling, sexual sins, alcohol, drugs, lying, stealing, pornography, and all of the other things that go along with these different topics are all a part of a sin problem. They are addictions, manifestations of what is really happening *on the inside* of our lives. You can medicate, counsel, or do all you want to try to overcome these things, but those means will not solve the heart of the issue because only God can fix this stuff, *this mess on the inside of us*. I am not saying that you shouldn't go to counseling; I support counseling. I am also not saying that you should never use medications or see a doctor; I also support supervised medicines and doctor visits. There is nothing wrong with either one. But, especially in America, I think we have become too accustomed to medicating our problems, our demons, instead of getting real help, real deliverance, and true healing from the Father. That should be the first step, and that is what it took to heal me.

## Getting Set Free

Getting delivered comes on God's own timing. If you remember in my story, I was the evil one and I was the one who drove Susie past

---

18. "The Top Most 5 Alarming Gambling Addiction Statistics," *Addictions*, accessed May 03, 2019, https://www.addictions.com/gambling/5-alarming-gambling-addic-tion-statistics/.

her breaking point. Even after I had an encounter with God, it still took Susie a while to be able to really trust me again. Looking back, it was the pornography after we were married that really caused the biggest problem. As I was doing it, I was also justifying it because of past sins I witnessed and heard about in the church. It was what I knew about the church people (some of the fallen pastors and "behind-door situations" that were coming out during that time) that allowed me to justify my sins over and over again. I would point to the corruption going on at a leadership level in order to try to justify my right to sin further. This doesn't work. It will only cause you to get involved so deep that you won't be able to climb out of it.

Remember the Prodigal Son in Luke 15:11–32? He had it all—all the comforts of his father's wealth and house. In addition, he had his father's love. He eventually ended up running away and blew his inheritance and life, ending up in the pig's pen: a big mess. He then ran back to his father, and of course his father welcomed him back. The only way to get out of the mess of our lives is to return to the Father's love.

## Time to Face the Facts

When we return to the Father's love, we have to lay down all our excuses—every last one. I couldn't keep pointing the finger at the pastor or other people I knew in the church who were doing bad things behind the scenes. I had to face the reality of the evil I had allowed back into my life and how it was affecting Susie. I will not go into details here, but Susie also went off the deep end to the point that I had to choose my sin or her: they would no longer be able to live with each other.

## Hosea 5: Repent and Turn to the Father

My "radical conversion" began when Jesus walked through a wall and spoke to me, an unforgettable experience which I go into in a later chapter. Within two weeks from the time He appeared to me, everything began to unfold at a rapid rate. However, even though I had had a breakthrough, I was still under demonic torment. Susie was now practicing the kind of life I had taught her, and she was sleeping around with some guy.

One day I borrowed a car from a friend to go find them. I knew about him and where he lived, so I went to his house and sat under the open window after midnight. I overheard them "doing the nasty." At this point, I was planning to scare them, but willing to shoot *him* if necessary. I held my 44 Magnum snug against my body and waited.

There I hid, underneath the window and listening to them. I was furious! All this stuff was going through my mind. After a brief moment, the Lord said, "You hear what's going on in there?" and I said, "Yes, Lord!" This is the same voice that talked to me two weeks earlier. At the time I called this voice "Mr. Love" because I didn't really recognize Him like I do now and I didn't know the Lord like I do now. Mr. Love said to me, "You consider what's going on in there sin?" I said, "Yes, I do." Then He said something to me that changed the course of my life. He said to me, "I don't hold this against her, I hold this sin against *you!*" Immediately, my grip on the gun loosed. God stopped me in my tracks.

I couldn't believe that she was in this man's house doing the nasty and God wasn't blaming her! Instead, He was holding it against *me!* Not only did this statement stop me, it stunned me. I went back to the car and drove back home. Once inside, I put the gun on the counter. Then I began talking to God because I didn't understand this statement at all. My mother always told me that if I couldn't back something up with scripture, then it may not be from God. So I took God at His Word and said to Him, "How can her sinful actions be held against me?" The Lord gave me Hosea 4:14. Curious, I had to go and look it up. It basically says that when your daughters commit harlotry and your wives commit adultery, I will not hold that against them because I hold it against you, men, the priest and leader of your home.

> "I will not punish your daughters when they commit
> harlotry, nor your brides when they commit adultery;
> for the **men** themselves go apart with harlots, and offer

sacrifices with a ritual harlot. Therefore people who do not understand will be trampled." (Hosea 4:14 NJKV)

My immediate thoughts were: *What on earth do I do with that? You're telling me I'm guilty and she's innocent? No way!* He spoke to me again, saying, "Did you repent for your sins two weeks ago when you met Me? Now it is time for you to repent for her sins as if they were yours. I'll remove them from *both* of you."

It was at this moment that I realized that I was the priest of my home. *I* was responsible for this mess and I was now "taking my rightful seat as the priest as my home"—that is, I was picking up the priesthood of my home and my rightful authority to my bloodline. I had led my family down the road of the sinful nature, and I had taught my wife how to become evil because of my addiction to pornography. I had been in adulterous relationships before, too, and now I was suddenly "Mr. Righteous" and thought I could hold Susie to a harsh standard without any mercy. Yet, because I was the spiritual leader of my home, the priest, God held her sin against me. This was the critical point of redeeming my bride.

This is also the critical point in redeeming the bride of Christ, because you can't redeem the wayward bride unless you take full responsibility for leading her in the wrong direction to begin with. The church must repent as a whole for forcing the bride of Christ to go in directions in which she never should have been led. As priests, we must be willing to repent for our sins and theirs (John 20). A priest's responsibility was to bring the proper sacrifice for the sins of the people; but in John 20:21–23, when Jesus first appeared to His disciples after the resurrection and breathed the Holy Spirit into them, He gave them His authority.

> Again Jesus said, "Peace be with you! As the Father has sent me, I am sending you." And with that he breathed on them and said, "Receive the Holy Spirit. If you forgive anyone's sins, their sins are forgiven; if you do not forgive them, they are not forgiven." (John 20:21–23)

If you forgive the sins of any, they are forgiven, but if you withhold forgiveness from any, it is withheld! Wow! It takes two to commit adultery, so was my wife committing adultery or were we both committing adultery? This is how it works: *If the two become one, then I was as guilty as she was.* This time with God became the turning point in my life. This is when I realized that I had to redeem the bride, my wife, the one I loved dearly. It was at this time that I had to learn to love and let go by letting God take full control in order to restore my messed-up life and family. I took responsibility for the sin that was being committed in my home and I repented for her sins, my family's sins, and my own sins. In these situations, it is love that covers a multitude of sins. That is what works. That is the *only* thing that works when your home has been torn apart.

> Above all, love each other deeply, because love covers
> over a multitude of sins. (1 Peter 4:8)

This ties into my next part: Hosea 5. In Hosea 5, Israel is once again being exposed for what that nation was doing—idolatry in all forms. The priests were just as guilty as the followers. They were doing things their way, and their pride was evident to God. They were allowing corruption in the community, in their own group and in the politicians, as well as in people's everyday lifestyles. Bottom line: They had turned from God, and God was now dealing with this issue. Through His judgment against them (the lion of Hosea 5:14–15), God would bring them to repentance in order for them to turn their hearts back to Him.

God judged me and did so rightly. This turned my sinful heart back to Him; and then I knew I would have to pursue my wife, the one who, at the time, had become what I didn't want her to be. But keep in mind that it was my fault. I had driven her to what she had become.

It's one thing to be the sinner and cause pain for someone else. It's something else entirely to be sinned against and have your trust broken. This is what had happened at that time in our lives. We were both so broken and shattered that we were now deliberately willing to hurt each other in our own sinful ways. Even so, God was bigger and better. He has a plan for every disaster that we can ever create. In Luke 4:18, Jesus says His purpose was to set the prisoner free. Most prisoners deserved to be in prison, but Jesus also said He came to set the captive free. Both find freedom in Christ.

## How Does This Apply to the Church?

The church wasn't designed to be a place of harm; it was created to be a place of healing. One of the most beautiful aspects of being Christlike is being able to watch the Lord heal the brokenhearted.

> He heals the brokenhearted and binds up their wounds.
> (Psalm 147:3)

There are many ways in which I could cover how my sin and what I created in my own life, our marriage, in Susie's heart, and within our business relate to the church, but I don't just want to point out the negative effects of sin. Instead, I would like to drive home one simple point: *What changed me the most was an actual personal encounter with God.* This was the single biggest, most life-changing moment in my life. My personal moments in which the Lord visited me have consistently changed my life. Were there people praying for me? Sure. Were there angels fighting for us at the time? Yes.

> For he will command his angels concerning you to guard
> you in all your ways. (Psalm 91:11)

Was God actively trying to get through to me by any means possible? I believe so—because He eventually did. What incredible mercy!

If God would radically pursue me, then I know He will pursue you and the people you love. Let's face it: There are people out there who are really facing some tough times. Awful situations. If God doesn't come through for them in the near future, it will all be over. Completely done. We have all been there. When you are walking through a really tough time in life, you realize pretty quickly just how badly we need God to respond to our SOS.

I want you to just think for a moment of all of the problems and situations you are currently facing right now. Got them yet? Some of you might need to create a list. Just pick the bigger problems. Next, I want you to think of as many serious problems as possible that you know about that concern your family or close friends. Maybe it is someone in the church who you know is going through a really hard time. Think of them too. You got them all? Pretty big list, huh? Next, I want you to multiply all your problems and the ones that you know about by the number of people who attend your church each week. If you have fourteen major problems or situations that come to your mind and 200 people who regularly attend your church each week, that is roughly 2,800 serious problems that God is actively working out right now. That doesn't include all the problems and serious situations that we *don't know about*. Sometimes, one single church can have very dire issues of which we are unaware going on just within the church leadership itself! If we multiply all this by all of the churches in the United States, how many problems in one day do you think we would have? Two or three million really serious problems or more? Who knows but God? And this only represents the local American Christian churches, not those around the world, or those relating to people *outside* of the church. Let's face it: we all have problems, and some are really big! My point is that God is *actively pursuing every person*. He is working to resolve what is dear to our hearts—things that only He can fix.

What the church needs right now is a divine encounter with God. The church needs what I was given. We need another awakening to stir our hearts and purify our lives from the sin that is the source of our problems. We need to be able to come into our local churches and be able to enter into the presence of God so that He can heal us. As a church, if we are not healed, we are not going to be able to heal others. Right now is a time for a divine awakening. The bride of Christ must rise, take her rightful place, and begin to exercise dominion over the earth until He returns. God hasn't called the church to be a bunch of cowards. He has called the church to be a powerful voice, a community of believers, a mighty army that invades every region of darkness.

> The weapons we fight with are not the weapons of the world. On the contrary, they have divine power to demolish strongholds. (2 Corinthians 10:4)

We can't fight battles if we are beat up as a church. We certainly can't *win* battles if we are broken before we even enter into warfare. It is time to be healed. It is more important than ever that we cut the cords of religion and regulation (forced intimacy) and open up the realm of true spiritual freedom within the body of Christ. This will require us, His church, to remove a lot of old wineskins in our personal lives.

# Chapter 7: God's Healing Plan for Sexual Abuse

The lot is cast into the lap, but its every decision is from
the Lord. (Proverbs 16:33)

We often forget that every step we take in life is a good step with the Lord. This is because God has an interesting way of creating God-centered outcomes, whether we walk foolishly or well. By now, you can easily tell that I took some really bad paths in life. My life was torn apart; my wife's life was torn apart; our company was falling apart, and so was our marriage. There isn't much left after that. My life reminded me of a country song. Country music can be depressing. If you really listen to some of the lyrics, you'll hear stuff like this: "I lost my wife, my job, my truck, and my dog; and now I am sitting on the couch with some Jack Daniels." This just doesn't sound fun to me. How about you? Sometimes the song just kept getting worse and more depressing the longer I played it. That was my life: the longer I tried to play it, the worse it got in my eyes ... but not God's. God had another perspective all along. At some point in our lives, we have all been there.

When I look back on the mess I created and then see what God did to restore my family, I humbly realize the power of Proverbs 16:33 above. It doesn't matter what is cast at your life—what matters is that it will not stand against you if the Lord doesn't want it to do that. He had a plan for me that kept my life in His hand; *He has a plan for you that will keep you in His hand as well.*

## Tough Choices

When we are in a mess, we have to make extremely tough choices. What is a choice? The word *choice* is defined as "an act of selecting or making a decision when faced with two or more possibilities" and "the right or ability to make, or possibility of making, such a selection."[19]

Speaking of choices, someone once said that "insanity is making the same choices over and over again and expecting different results." This is true in spiritual matters. This is also true when it comes to healing. When it is time to emotionally and sexually heal, it is time to change forever. If you are reading this and you know that it is time for healing, then you know it is time for a lifestyle change.

## Healing Requires One to Let Go

Some of you will have to permanently close some doors so you never go back there again. I had to close the door on the fact that I was raped at the age of seven. I had to allow God to heal my life emotionally and spiritually when it came to that tragedy. I had to accept what had happened and that I couldn't change it. I also had to surrender my hatred of Sylvan Bishop. What he did to me was not right; it was pure evil. I never talked to him about it when I was around him or his family or as I got older, but internally, deep inside, I had to let him go. I had to forgive him. Say what? Forgive the person who raped you? *Yes*! I had to forgive him in order for me to go free. Forgiveness did *not* mean that I ever would trust him again; it just meant that I let him go in my heart in order to move on. I laid the whole thing at the feet of Jesus.

Let's talk about this a little bit. We have to let go, but how do we know what to do next with that relationship? God gives us guidelines about dealing with someone who is in sin. This verse sort of gives us all a safety net when we are dealing with several serious issues at once. Sexual, physical, and emotional abuses are all very serious. Here is where we start:

---

19. "Choice," Google Search, accessed May 03, 2019, https://www.google.com/search?-client=firefox-b-1&q=choices definition.

"If your brother sins against you go and rebuke him in private. If he listens to you, you have won your brother. But if he won't listen, take one or two more with you, so that by the testimony of two or three witnesses every fact may be established. If he pays no attention to them, tell the church. But if he doesn't pay attention even to the church, let him be like an unbeliever and tax collector to you." (Matthew 18:15–17)

This passage is referring to a believer-versus-believer conflict. It is not referring to someone you don't know who physically attacked you. It is not saying you should go and find your unknown rapist or attacker and set them straight. Going back to someone who raped you isn't a good idea. Remember that this is Matthew 18, an Old Covenant people with an Old Covenant language. Fast-forward to when Jesus grafted the Gentiles into the family and made a tax collector part of his ministry team. Know that is the gospel, the good news of the kingdom, but there are still boundaries. A powerful book that I would suggest reading for more on this topic is *Forgiveness* by Rodney Hogue.

However, this passage from Matthew 18 is saying that offenses must be addressed. If the person doesn't change their ways, then the Bible says to have nothing to do with that person ever again. It goes even further to say that you should treat them as an unbeliever (an outcast) or a tax collector. (Back then, you didn't trust unbelievers and you surely didn't trust tax collectors.) This is what *letting go* looks like sometimes. In order to let go, you must forgive them, but *forgiveness does not mean that you trust them again.*

In like manner, you may forgive your attacker, but that doesn't mean that you go on a second date with them. You don't confront them alone in a dark alley. There is a big difference between trust and forgiveness.

It is important to understand that we must forgive the person that did us wrong. What if someone that you know, maybe a trusted friend at work, takes advantage of you when you were drinking or unable to defend yourself? What would you do?

I never stayed connected to Sylvan at all. He ended up in jail and later died there. I never got to tell him that I had forgiven him, but in my heart, I let him go. I chose to forgive him and moved on. This is what we have to do.

## Healing Has to Love Enough to Confront

Confrontation! Who likes it? Most people don't. If you had the choice between sitting and quietly reading a book, fishing, hiking, watching TV, or getting into a serious confrontation for the next two hours, which one would you choose? Most are going to want to do anything else but confront someone. Not fun. But it has to be done. When we get involved with sexual or physical abuse, alcoholism, or drugs, something will snap and something bad will always come out of that. This type of behavior will always destroy a marriage, relationship, and a person's life.

> The thief comes only to steal and kill and destroy; I have come that they may have life, and have it to the full. (John 10:10)

The devil will never stop stealing, killing, and destroying people's lives. The bottom line is that the devil wants to kill you. He wants to destroy your life, your family, and everyone around you. And he will use any means he can find to do that. So when we encounter an abusive situation, we have to first understand that the devil is in the center of it. I am not saying that "the devil made me do it!" The devil didn't tell me to do all of the bad things I did; I chose to do them. But the devil certainly loved it! My point is that we can't blame God for the actions that we do and the messes that we find ourselves in.

When someone is endangered or harmed, love has to be tough enough to confront and require change. Without it, you will be stuck in that mess for the long term. Sometimes we have to walk away and give the person and situation over to the Lord. Other times, we have to address the problem and this can be really difficult to do. Forgiveness is tough. Forgiveness can be the hardest part of the whole abusive situation. Believe me, I have been there.

## Healing Demands Acceptance

Let me paint a picture for you. I was walking with God in Vero Beach. I knew that I was hearing the Lord and that I had my priorities straight. I had an encounter with God during this time. He said, "You need to make a choice. If you choose to stay here in Vero Beach any longer, I will prosper your business. I will prosper you, but I cannot promise you, your wife, or your marriage. If you move to Deltona, Florida, I promise you your marriage, your wife, and your children. I'll never leave you nor forsake you, but I will not make it easy on you. I will use you to preach the gospel if you trust Me." Of course, I chose to go to Deltona and God kept all His promises. I had to accept what I had done and what had been done to me, though. Through doing that, I chose to move on for the better of the whole. *Healing will require something from you.* Usually this includes accepting what has happened, letting it go, and moving on.

## Healing Begins with a Choice

At one point, before I was really healed, I was disillusioned. I felt overwhelmed by my sin and the demonic strongholds attached to it. I was an emotional and mental wreck. I was losing my business; I was losing everything. God was allowing me to be stripped down to nothing in order for Him to reveal the core of all of it. It was during this time that I wanted to shoot that guy who was with Susie. Susie had become what I was just starting to get delivered from—broken! She was the one who was out and about because I pushed her past her limits in life. At that point, she didn't care if we stayed married or not. So, one day I was at the wrong place at the wrong time and decided that I was going to deal with this problem head-on. I was going to shoot someone who was with Susie that day. Why? I had also had it. I was past the breaking point too—the same place to which I had driven Susie.

During this time, God said things to me like, "Listen, she's just releasing her pain." But I was going through a great deal of pain as well. Thankfully, I chose to hand my anger and hate over to God.

That day—once I laid the gun down, and once I laid my life down—I really found out who God was. Oh sure, I knew God. I mean, come on: I grew up as a deacon's kid and went to church every week regularly. I had encounters with God, too, but *it wasn't until I surrendered my choices to His will that I really found God.* I found out that He wanted to walk with me for who I was: His son, His friend, His child.

I had a relationship with Him now, not just a one-way street where I was playing church and playing around with evil relationships at the same time. I was willing to serve God with or without Susie, with and without my business. I would serve God, with and without everything, in order to have Him. When I became willing to serve God *without* her, then God told me He could trust me *with* her. This is how I got my wife back. This is how I got everything back.

I had to let it all go. I had to be willing to lay everything down to follow Him—regardless. The *regardless* part of following the Lord is the toughest, in my opinion. It is what makes or breaks our relationship with our Father. It's what really counts. Many are willing to follow Christ as long as they have money, or are rich, or have it their way in life. This isn't how it works, though.

> "All these I have kept since I was a boy," [the rich man] said. When Jesus heard this, he said to him, "You still lack one thing. Sell everything you have and give to the poor, and you will have treasure in heaven. Then come, follow me." When he heard this, he became very sad, because he was very wealthy. Jesus looked at him and said, "How hard it is for the rich to enter the kingdom of God! Indeed, it is easier for a camel to go through the eye of a needle than for someone who is rich to enter the kingdom of God." (Luke 18:21–25)

The *regardless* part in this passage is when Jesus told the rich man to become poor in order to truly learn to trust Him and become "kingdom rich." Kingdom rich is when we put our trust and effort into the Lord's kingdom instead of ours. This is the *regardless* part. As followers of Christ, we have to get past the *regardless* part. This means that when we put our hate and bad circumstances in the Father's hands, He deal with them His way. We have to trust Him, *regardless of the outcome.* This may mean that your attacker goes free. This may mean that other serious consequences emerge from the fact that you were attacked (like STDs). This may mean that your life is forever changed, but *regardless,* we have to learn to hand it over to God and trust Him. This is what I had to do first. This is what Susie had to do later—and she did.

## Healing Starts with Jesus—Light of the World

By August of 1993, Susie and I had been married around fifteen years, and I was still a *Christian jerk.* I was trying to play the Christian, but I was really being a big jerk more than anything else! By now, she was messing up, I was messing up, and we were really starting to hate each other. But keep in mind, I was the abuser and now I was feeling abused. You know the old saying, "What comes around goes around"?

Well, it came around, but God wasn't giving up on either of us.

About three weeks before the life-changing encounter with God (the one where God was going to let hell have its way with me), Susie actually left me. She went and stayed at her mom's house, just to get away from me. That was a wake-up call from the Lord that I didn't listen to. I could have repented that night, but I chose not to. Once again, things were getting worse for me and Susie.

At two o'clock in the morning, God met me. The lights were on in the kitchen, which was adjacent to the bedroom. The pool room was dark because there were no lights in there, and it sat between the kitchen and the bedroom. I had been under deep conviction for about a month before this encounter in my house near the pool table. That's right! God visited me.

I saw the power of God right there in my house; and I knelt down at the pool table, my pool table in Vero Beach, Florida, and prayed. It went something like this: "If You're the God of my mother, then You have supernatural power. She said You had enough power that You could convert and change a man's heart. If You're that God, I'll serve You, but I'm not making another promise until You change my heart."

Then I said, "I am a liar, I am a thief. I am a whore-monger and I am an abuser. I have an evil heart. If You can't give me a new heart, I will not make another commitment to You. I am done making commitments that I can't keep. I need a new heart." That was the most honest prayer I could have ever prayed. I stood up from that pool table, stopped praying, and nothing happened.

And this thought went through my mind: *God, I just gave You everything that I have in that prayer. I can't give You any more than that. If you can't respond to that, I don't know that I can serve You.* Little did I know that His timing and response would be perfect. I turned around and took two steps toward the kitchen when lightning struck the room. A bolt of light literally entered the room against the wall. It was still around two in the morning, so the room had been very dark. All of sudden, there was this blinding light instead. It was a bright light, powerful like lightning. Extremely bright! It was as if a flame had shot through the building or something. But it wasn't a flame or a lightning strike; it was Jesus, showing up in my house.

Jesus walked out of this bright, blinding light. He walked out of the light and stood in front of me, piercing me with His eyes. They were like a real liquid love of fire. Still staring at me, He put His hand out and said, "Charles Layton Coker Jr. Tonight you will choose who you will serve. Put your hand in My hand. I'll never leave you nor forsake you—or I will let hell have its way with you." Then He pointed and hell opened up. I heard hell; I smelled hell. I could literally hear the screams of hell. He said, "I will let hell have its way with you, but tonight, you must choose who you're going to serve." Right there in that empty house next to the pool table, I chose Jesus. In an instant, I had a supernatural conversion, and received a new heart. I truly was changed forever.

## Healing Requires Cleanup Time

When all of this happened, it really freaked me out! I knew instantly that God had delivered me from alcohol and pornography. I took a huge duffel bag and filled it full of pornography, and I dumped all the alcohol in the house down the drain. I had a pack of cigarettes because I was a smoker, and I thought, *I can't quit smoking too—all at the same time! That would be too much too fast!* I reached for the cigarettes, and God audibly spoke to me and said, "How small do you think I am?" I fell to the ground, crying, and crumbled up the cigarettes right then.

The next thing I did was call my dad. I said, "Dad, I've given my life back to Christ. I'm sorry to say that there's not a Bible in my house to wake up to anymore. Could you bring me a Bible?" God had given me a new heart, and He put a love in my heart like I'd never had before.

## Healing Will Determine Your Future

During this time I kept experiencing encounters with God. He said to me, "I want to show you your future. It will give you something to hold on to." (Notice that God wants to give us something to hold on to after we have let go of everything we had.)

What he showed me next was breathtaking. He showed me a marriage ceremony with twenty couples renewing their vows. Susie and I were one of those couples. Right after the marriage scene, I saw myself standing in front of ten thousand people, sharing my story and preaching the gospel. He gave me some promises:

He told me that these were my *key* promises.

*Number one*: Your marriage will be restored.

*Number two*: You will stand before thousands of people and tell them just how good I am.

God has a plan for your life too. When the healing occurs, He will help you see a better, stronger future. It doesn't matter what you went through; what matters is that you went through it and you're coming out on the other side now. He has a future glory for us that surpasses all of our present and past sufferings.

> I consider that our present sufferings are not worth comparing with the glory that will be revealed in us. (Romans 8:18)

## The Crisis between God, Women, and Me

Being afraid of women became a crisis between me and the living God I was serving. This happened within two or three weeks after Jesus came through the wall, and I knew I had truly been born again. I knew He had called me, but I was still going through a lot. Eventually I came to the conclusion that I should ask God to release me from my marriage so Susie could find somebody who would not ever hurt her again. I was simply consumed with not damaging her anymore. For three days, I argued with God, saying, "Please release me! You can't trust me. I'm not trustworthy." Even so, things changed because God told me He could make me trustworthy! Again, my initial thought was, *No, You can't. I'm a scumbag. I will cheat. I will do it. I know it's not who I really am and I don't want to, but I will because I know me.*

During this conversation I was resting in bed and arguing with God. God replied, "What if I guaranteed that you would never ever touch another woman inappropriately? What if I guaranteed that you would only ever touch your wife? Do you want Me to heal your marriage?" I answered, "You could guarantee me?" Then He said to me, "I am God! I could make you never touch another woman inappropriately." It was obvious who trusted who. I know I didn't trust me, but I did trust God. In fact, I think God trusted me more than I trusted Him. Remember, *God sees where we will be before we get there.*

God told me to place my Bible on the floor, get out of bed, and stand on it. So I got out of bed and stood on top of my Bible. While standing on the Bible, God told me to raise my arms and surrender. Here's what He said: "Charles Layton Coker Jr. If you ever touch another woman inappropriately, I will kill you stone dead." Bam! The fear of God hit me; and I'm telling you, I have never had a thought about touching another woman inappropriately since.

## Healing Removes Fear

That fear of touching another woman wrongfully kept me from communicating with any woman. I wouldn't be caught dead around a woman. I wouldn't be caught close to a woman without a group of people around me. I would barely hug a woman. I just avoided women. After about seven years of this, God healed me of any fear of being around women.

> There is no fear in love. But perfect love drives out fear, because fear has to do with punishment. The one who fears is not made perfect in love. (1 John 4:18)

## Healing Will Reveal God's Promises

I feared women more than men. Why? God told me that if I ever cheated or touched another woman wrongfully again that He would kill me. Therefore, I avoided women if at all possible. I avoided them like a plague from Egypt; but deep inside I still struggled with the fact that in the back of my mind, I knew that if the right woman came along and stripped naked in front of me, I would get tempted. I also knew that if I got strongly tempted, I might bite the apple. I knew that I still had a core issue of feeling that I was not trustworthy. I was asking God to release me from that. I feared that with my record, I was going to cheat again one day, and I wanted to be free of that.

Bottom line: I had a crazy sex drive. It was ramped up like high-octane gas. Back then, it was haunting me to the point I felt that I couldn't control it. I had to place this passion for sex on the altar. It happened was when I was in the shower. God asked me to give this sex drive to Him, so I knelt down in the shower. I literally took my tormenting sex life, handed it to God, and put it on the altar. What happened? He took it because I gave it to Him! He said, "If you'll give it to Me and let it be under My authority, I'll give you the freedom that you need." From that moment on, I did not get an erection for almost a year. Seriously! Men, can you imagine this?

Anyway, back to the shower. When I came out of the shower, Jesus walked into the bathroom with a robe and said, "You've given Me the thing that tormented you the most. You put it under My authority. I'm going to heal you in this area that you put out of balance, and now you must wear this." Then He put a robe of righteousness on me. Righteousness will bring sexual lust into balance.

In 1993, Susie moved home for Christmas for the boys, and the Lord spoke to me and said that she would never leave again. All along Susie had been telling me that it was over and she was going to leave me, but God's word to me was true; and of course, Susie never left again. The next year, we went to my mom and dad's church. It was Valentine's Day, February 14, and the pastor got up and said, "You know, today's Valentine's Day! Anybody who wants to renew their marriage vows can come forward." Well, it didn't take us long. I got up there, but Susie only did it to get me off her rear: I had been hounding her to do this. (By this time, I was fanatically serving God and she was still fighting with religion as far as she was concerned.) When we got up there, guess how many couples there were? Twenty! It was at this event that God told me to never mention divorce again in our marriage.

## Healing Releases Commitment

We were back together, and things were finally healing between us. Months passed, and then years. God had made it clear to both of us who He is and what He wanted from us. We were getting our lives together as best we could. We were both trying, and it was during this latter part of our marriage that I actually feared women for so long.

After my shower experience, I didn't think I'd ever have sex again. Even when I was lying in bed with my wife, I would be holding her and that was all I could do for one solid year—just hold her. I would remind

Him that it was a long time to not be able to have any sex with the one you loved and that we were legally married. Nevertheless, for one year! God reminded me who was in charge of this sexual healing thing that I had asked Him for. During this time, God healed both of us sexually. We both needed a deep healing. I told Susie that this was what God was doing when I held her. He was healing us of all the past encounters, the affairs and abuses—all of it. He was divinely healing us in a way that only He could do. Sexual healing is a very personal healing and God has the master plan for that.

## How Does This Apply to the Church?

The church is in a state of constant healing. There are always things happening to people in the church. In order for the people in the church to heal, we have to teach them how to heal and learn to consistently walk in the power of healing. As ministers, we must be willing to let God work in our church services anytime He chooses. This can be tough because sometimes we have an amazing message that we put a lot of time into, and God will choose to go in another direction instead.

We also have to be open in allowing the Holy Spirit to work through whomever He chooses. There isn't anything wrong with the same preacher speaking every Sunday; but sometimes I think we need to step aside and let the Lord work through other people. Sometimes, someone in the congregation needs to hear a word from the Lord from someone else. This also allows another person to exercise their gift in preaching, so it is good for the church in general.

Until the church surrenders its will for the Lord's will to heal, we will not see the healings at the level God desires. There is no substitute for the presence of God in our everyday lives. As Christians, we have to learn how to display His presence—in the church and outside the walls of the church too. This is obedience. When we have this, the Lord is welcome to work in any way that He chooses.

# Chapter 8: How God Healed Rape (Susie's Story)

## Meeting Charlie

I t has taken a long time to finally write our story. I have shared it many times behind pulpits, but never written it down. My story, like so many others out there, is too often told at a much later time in someone's life. Why? It's because it is about being raped. No one wants to go through it; and afterward, no one wants to talk about it. For me, it was something that just happened; and at the time there wasn't anything I could do about it. I knew I had to continue in life, and so I did. At sixteen, I had to learn how to survive in a different way, as a different person now, but still the same me.

> Direct me in the path of your commands, for there I find delight. (Psalm 119:35)

I've always been a pretty simple kind of girl; I was just dumb and young. I'm not sure if I was fourteen or fifteen at the time, but Charlie and I went to the same church and I saw him in youth group. I had a crush on him, but he was two years older than me. We were just the kind of kids that were the attracted to each other and I think it was pretty normal.

It was teen stuff then. It's the same old game today, but there's just a different playing field now—and a whole new set of rules. Charlie had a car, like a lot of boys his age. We didn't have cell phones and all of the stuff people have these days, so getting a car for a young man was a big deal—probably a bigger deal than it is today. Other friends of mine also had cars, so I wasn't one of those girls who had to have a man that had a car. The car didn't matter to me at all. I liked Charlie, regardless.

Charlie's parents were leaders in our church. Charlie wasn't there all the time, but he was there enough for me to notice. He was working in the sound booth in the same youth hall that I was in regularly. He was a typical kid, goofing off sometimes but also getting the work done. He wasn't causing a bunch of trouble, but some considered him trouble in the youth group. I wouldn't say that he was perfect or anything. Charlie was just a typical teenager and I had a crush on him.

## My Background

I was brought up as a Christian in a Christian home. I had three older sisters and an older brother. Around this time, my older brother was preparing to go off to the navy, and both my parents were active in church. My mom taught Sunday school and helped out in other ways too. I wasn't allowed to go to movies or school dances or football games. Football games and movies and all of those kinds of activities were considered "devil stuff." If it wasn't associated with the church or the church youth, I couldn't do it or even think of being a part of it. In the summertime, I spent my time at summer camps and vacation Bible schools. That is how I was raised. But being young and like most typical church girls, who could be a little mischievous and just wanting to get out and have fun, I sometimes told my parents that I was going to a church event or something like that; and Charlie and I went parking instead. Let me define "parking" for you: We didn't have sex. We would kiss and make out. "Making out" wasn't like hooking up is today.

## Then and Now

Like today, kids are going to be kids. A lot of parents think that if they send their kids to Christian school or just keep them in a bubble at church that bad things won't happen to them. But they do anyway. Bad situations came up back then among church kids and are still happening today. We have to place our kids in the hands of God and trust Him for their care. (I personally homeschooled one of my sons and the other graduated from to a Christian school. Believe me, there is no such thing as a Christian bubble!)

Back then in the youth group when we were growing up, I wasn't really looking to find a boyfriend to date, I wasn't allowed to date anybody. I didn't go out on dates or even go to the movies with the boys. As I have mentioned, I couldn't go to school dances, which were really popular back then because there wasn't a whole lot to do, so my circle of friends was small and primarily made up of the youth group.

## The Day It All Happened

It was 1977, and it was Charlie's eighteenth birthday. I was about three days shy of my sixteenth birthday. Charlie's parents were out of town and he invited some people over to his house after church. I went over there with some friends that evening, and we were all sitting around talking and having fun. I didn't consider Charlie a really bad person at the time. Truthfully, I was just really naive.

After a while, Charlie and I went into the bedroom and started making out. (Again, hugging and kissing, not sex. I didn't go in that bedroom that day with the intention of having sex.) After a while, he forced himself on me and that was the end of that. I walked into his bedroom a virgin and walked out not one. I was naive; better put, I was a silly dumb little girl just like most of us were back then. Whatever else I was, I was devastated.

Some might ask, did you call the cops? Did you get a rape test? A what? I didn't know what a rape kit was back then because they didn't exist. DNA testing? What was that? Our culture was extremely different back then. We came out of the room and sat around for a while. A short time later, Charlie took me to a friend's house and I hung out there for a while because I wasn't ready to go home yet. *I didn't tell anyone.* Things were different back then. They weren't like they are now. Some women have to suppress such a violent thing for years or most of their lives. Some just can't talk about it and don't want to. It took me years to openly discuss this.

Even after the attack, I never talked to Charlie about it either. I just went about life. It was what I had to do to cope and deal with it. Sometimes it is best to let the Lord do His work in a person on His timing and that had to be my reasoning back then.

## First Time—First Pregnancy

As I mentioned before, I didn't say anything to anyone, including my parents about what happened to me that night. As things moved on, though, I was four and a half months pregnant and starting to show a little bit. I remember going to school. I don't know how, but my friends didn't know that I was pregnant. One day I was taking a nap and the phone rang and my mom answered the phone. To this day I don't know who told her, but someone called my mom and said these exact words: "Susie's pregnant!" and hung up. That changed everything because up to that day I never thought about being pregnant. I just went about my life because it was what I knew how to do at the time. I was sixteen years old.

My mother came to me in my room. She never raised her voice.

She only wanted to know two things: Who was it, and was there alcohol involved (was he drunk)?

I told her it was Charlie, but I didn't tell her that he raped me. After my mom got off the phone and talked to me alone, she told my dad. That night after he got off of work, my dad came into my room and said to me, "I'm sorry this happened to you, but I'll stand by you." This meant the world to me at the time. I had great support from my parents. That great support is how I got through it.

Parents, sometimes it is best to support your kids, regardless of how you feel and this can be really hard sometimes. Because of their help, I made it through one of the toughest stages of my life. My parents were amazing to walk through something like that the way that they did.

## I Will Choose to Press On

About five months into the pregnancy, I quit school to go to night school. The good news is that I didn't have morning sickness or anything like that, so that helped. I eventually got a GED; and during that time, I kept going to the same church. There I was—going to the same church, but now pregnant. I didn't tell though; I never told anyone that I had been raped. Some people talked about me behind my back and stuff like that. I could tell. The pastors were fabulous at that church. They helped me through that tough time in my life as well.

Eventually, my mom talked to one of the pastors, and the pastor called Charlie into his office in order to ask him to help out with the hospital expenses. Yep! That comes with pregnancy. At that time, health insurance didn't cover all the stuff that it does now. Charlie went into the pastor's office to have this meeting; and once the pastor brought up the topic about my baby, Charlie said, "It's not mine!" and got up and walked out.

In fact, Charlie didn't want anything to do with what had happened during my entire pregnancy, delivery, and all of it. For the first eighteen months after Jason was born, Charlie wasn't around or involved with us at all. I had a friend who worked at Wendy's, and one day Charlie went through the drive-through. As he was going through, my friend wrote, "Congratulations on your son." I believe that's probably how he found out Jason had been born. God's hand can be found in some of the littlest things in life. I don't know the full motive as to why my friend wrote that on his napkin, but I do know that God was in the details of how this mess unfolded to allow the Lord to put everything back into its proper plan. Sometimes we don't see it; we don't see the divine plan of a sovereign Creator. God created, and He is still creating good out of all that we have destroyed. This is who He is: a Redeemer.

> For you created my inmost being; you knit me together
> in my mother's womb. (Psalm 139:13)

91

## Why Didn't God Warn Me?

I would like to address something concerning Christians and rape. Some reading this might wonder, *Why didn't God warn me about Charlie or stop me from going over there that night? Why couldn't God have sent an angel to stop this from happening? Why didn't God give me a scripture or warn my parents about it in a dream the night before? After all, you were a Christian.* Yes, I was a Christian, and I was raped. I was helpless to defend myself that night. Sometimes bad things happen in life whether we are Christian or not. Sometimes good people die in horrible car accidents, or they survive with very serious problems to their bodies that they have to cope with for the rest of their lives. It isn't because God is a bad person or because He has no desire to protect those He loves. Instead, it is because we live in a broken and sinful world filled with broken people. Until the Lord returns to fix it once and for all, we are going to continue to see and be around evil.

At sixteen years old, I somehow processed this and I never blamed God for getting raped or pregnant. When bad things happen to us, we are often too quick to blame God. God's rain falls on the just and the unjust at the same time.

## Aftermath

It wasn't until about thirty years later that I could actually share this story and tell people about it in public. Looking back, I just put it out of my mind. I didn't really even think about it. Obviously, with our relationship starting out on the wrong foot like this, there were going to be some serious repercussions at some point. And there were; there were some really tough times in our marriage in the next ten-year span.

At one time, Charlie was deep into pornography and it was like the sexual abuse coming up all over again. I was going to leave him and walk out of his life for good. He was getting deeper and deeper into more sin, and I couldn't take it anymore. I was going way out there into the deep end myself. Everything was falling apart. There might have been other reasons behind Charlie's actions, but I couldn't take it anymore.

I want to point something out here. Sometimes we go off on the deep end because we are done. Something inside of us snaps and we lose it. That was the case with me. I just couldn't take going through something like all that again. Interestingly, God knew that I was going to snap. After years of broken promises from Charlie, telling me that he was going to change, my trust was completely broken. At first I only felt the lack of security in our marriage, but then one day it became a reality. I was done with it, and I turned my heart to others to take away the loneliness and cover the pain. The love was gone. I just wanted to be loved, and I definitely was not getting my needs met from Charlie. We use the word *snap* like it was a surprise, but it was not a surprise. I just made a choice that I was done.

We forget that God is so much bigger than our worries. He knows the end from the beginning. The woman at the well (John 4:1–42) was a good example. While Jesus was talking to her, He brought up that she had had many husbands and that the guy presently with her was not her husband. However, that was not the primary thing Jesus cared about. He cared most that she stopped that lifestyle and turned from sin. Getting her life turned around was the most important thing on Jesus's mind. For you and me, that is still the most important thing on Jesus's mind. He wants to turn our lives around for the better. He wants to pull us out of lifestyles that will harm us and, eventually, kill us.

When I snapped and wanted to leave Charlie, God knew that "snapping" the way I did was better than other ways. He knew it and helped me through it. This is how God works. He will always meet you where you are, because God knows your breaking point. Every one of us has a breaking point, even as Christians. He knows how much you can take and what you can walk through.

### Prayer Works

That sixteen-year-old girl who got pregnant years ago wanted the dad, Charlie, in her son's life. I prayed that Charlie would be in Jason's life growing up, and God heard me. He answered my prayer, but it did not turn out exactly how I thought it would. God's ways are so much better than ours. Sometimes He is answering our prayers and we don't even see it.

## Truth Hurts!

So, there I was, a rape victim, now pregnant, back in the day before DNA and ultrasounds, not even knowing if I was having a boy or girl and still in night school, attempting to now get my GED. My life had really changed, and I never asked for that, but I chose to handle it. Sometimes we are given stuff in life that we didn't ask for, but we must choose to deal with it.

One area that became apparent to me back then was that, deep inside, I still cared for Charlie. I still respected his parents and family. They had nothing to do with this; Charlie did. Word eventually got out that I said the baby was Charlie's. How did I know this? Well, that was easy: Charlie was the only one I had ever been with. Sums that up! Charlie was telling people (like our pastors) that the baby wasn't his.

Charlie's mom and dad were having the youth over to their house for an evening. Evidently, Becky (Charles's sister) asked her mom if she was going to invite me over, and Charlie's mom said, "I'm not inviting her here." But something happened, and that something was the divine conviction and leading of the Holy Spirit. The Lord knew that I was innocent and I was not going around attempting to cause trouble or defame a person or a family's name. Others may not have known the full truth at the time, including Charlie's mother. She didn't know all of the details surrounding my pregnancy because I chose not to tell anyone. However, our pastors did know that Charlie was the father of my baby, but I never shared that he had raped me. I am sure it was through them that Charlie's parents eventually found out that they had a grandson but could not openly approve of the situation.

On that night, God worked out something that I will never forget. One of my friends who was there at Charlie's house with the rest of us went into Charlie's room and stole one of his pictures out of his bedroom. He later gave it to me so I could put it into a book for my son. Now my son would have a picture of who his father was. This was the crazy stuff that I was walking through then, and God was watching out for me through it.

## First Time Sex, First Time Raped, First Time Pregnant—Three In One!

There I was: an innocent, sixteen-year-old, naive girl. I had had sex for the first time, because I was raped, and I was now pregnant all in one moment on one evening with a guy I had liked from my youth group. Soon, a child would be on the way; and two years later, I would marry the person who had raped me and given me that child at sixteen. To add a greater twist to this storyline, we would become ministers. And now we pastor a church.

Doesn't this sound like something you would find in a tabloid magazine or a soap opera? Most normal people are asking, "What on earth were you thinking, Susie? Why didn't you tell someone what he did?" Most would probably scream "Kill him!" or something like that.

This is what I want to address for a moment. This is the most important part of this whole chapter: *I chose to forgive*, regardless. I want to talk about forgiveness for a moment.

> This is my blood of the covenant, which is poured out for
> many for the forgiveness of sins. (Matthew 26:28)

This verse is about when Jesus took the cup and gave thanks, then said that His blood was given for the forgiveness of sins. Jesus was referring to Exodus 24.

> Moses then took the blood, sprinkled it on the people
> and said, "This is the blood of the covenant that the Lord
> has made with you in accordance with all these words."
> (Exodus 24:8)

When Jesus said this, the Jews would have known that He was saying, "I am He. I am the One who made the covenant with you back in Exodus 24:8, and I am the One making a covenant with you now for the removal of your sins." He was also saying, "And by the way, I am the final and official sacrifice. I am going to the cross once and for all. No more sacrifices will follow after Me."

Real forgiveness is only found in Jesus Christ and Him alone. It isn't found through any other way on earth. First and foremost, we need to find forgiveness for *our* sins, not the sins of the one who abused us, attacked us, or raped us—but *our* sins! If you are not born again, now is the time to ask Jesus to forgive you of your sins and yours alone!

> Truly I tell you, if anyone says to this mountain, "Go, throw yourself into the sea," and does not doubt in their heart but believes that what they say will happen, it will be done for them. Therefore I tell you, whatever you ask for in prayer, believe that you have received it, and it will be yours. And when you stand praying, if you hold anything against anyone, forgive them, so that your Father in heaven may forgive you your sins. (Mark 11:23–26)

How does this passage relate to you forgiving? If we are *not* walking in power, then we haven't forgiven. Forgiveness activates the power to change and move mountains.

Secondly, we must also forgive the person who abused us or did wrong to us. Whether you know the person, like I did, or not. Maybe you see that person every day or each week, like I did at the time. Or perhaps you don't even know this person or see them at all. Maybe you don't even know your attacker's name or have any idea what happened to you that day. *Regardless*, it doesn't matter. What matters is the fact that someone wronged you. Maybe they beat you up, raped you, stole from you, lied about you, or abused you: the list can go on and on. Maybe some of you need to list all the people who wronged you and then write why or how they hurt you next to their name. After you are finished with listing all of the people who hurt you, or even just that one single person who hurt you the most—maybe raped you, even—you need to forgive them. *What? Forgive them?!*

This is the toughest part. Sometimes this might be even more unbearable than the abuse, attack, or rape. Forgiveness can be one of the toughest parts of life because in our natural heart of hearts, we want to hate, we want to repay, and we want to cause harm to the person who harmed us. This is normal; it is completely natural to want to hurt the person that once hurt you. God understands this. He has been watching the cycles of revenge being played out since the first murder in the Bible, when Cain killed Abel in Genesis 4:1–16.

The current hatred or anger that you might have toward the person who abused you is natural, it is normal, and God knows about it. And He understands. Do you think someone wants to be raped? Don't you think for one moment that thousands of thoughts went through my mind from the time it happened to me until I found peace with God about it? *Yes! They did!* Was I angry, confused about what was going on, and all of that other stuff back then? Yes. But I dealt with it. I knew I had to deal with it and grow up, become I was a mom when I was sixteen, and I never asked to be one.

> "The Spirit of the Lord is on me, because he has anointed me to proclaim good news to the poor. He has sent me to proclaim freedom for the prisoners *and captives* and recovery of sight for the blind, to set the oppressed free."
> (Luke 4:18)

I love how this scripture reads. You see, a prisoner *belongs* in jail. No matter how or why they got there, their home is jail. A captive, regardless of how they became captive, is a prisoner because of someone else's vice, evil, or sin. But Christ sets *both* the prisoner and the captive free! He breaks all chains, opens all prisons, and releases the captives.

Sometimes we just don't get dealt what we want, but it is most important to deal with the heart of the issue. As painful and bizarre as it is, you must forgive the person you hate the most. You must forgive the person who raped you, abused you, stole from you, or whatever. If I can do it, so can you.

> But if you do not forgive others their sins, your Father will not forgive your sins. (Matthew 6:15)

The word *forgiveness* in Matthew 6:15 means "to pardon, let go, walk away, abandon, or leave behind."[20] In other words, you (myself included) must leave behind, walk away, and move on. This is what God is asking us to do.

I want to point out something else. Forgiveness does *not* mean that you trust that person again. It is one thing to forgive; it is something else to become their best friend, trust them with your life, and have a business or build a relationship with them again. Forgiveness means to *let them go* and give them to God in your heart. It doesn't mean that they shouldn't pay for the pain or crime that they committed. A lot of people think that if someone gets raped and the victim forgives the attacker, they should do nothing at all. This is not the case. You, the victim, are asked by God to forgive the attacker, the rapist. *This does not mean that you shouldn't report it.* And if you forgive that person, this does not promise that they won't do it again to someone else. The purpose of you forgiving the person who harmed you is for you. Forgiveness helps us find peace with God, as well as the healing that only God can offer.

The Lord warned us about judging other in Mathew 7:1–2. God told Charlie one day that God was a righteous Judge and that there should only be one judge on each case, so if Charlie was judging someone, God would not.

The person who raped you may never change. They may never go to jail or be punished for what they did. That isn't on you; that is on them. But *regardless*, we don't have the responsibility of holding hatred in our hearts. We have the responsibility of forgiving in our hearts, and this forgiveness has nothing to do with the outcome of the person who

---

20. Gregory A. Lint and Brian D. Rogers, *The Complete Biblical Library* (Springfield, MO: World Library Press, 1997), 502.

attacked you or me. Forgiveness means that you walked away and let them go in your heart, and that you no longer hate the person that hurt you the most.

## How Does This Relate to the Church?

One statistic suggests that roughly 25 percent of Americans attend church three times in two months. In actual fact, "only 23-25% of Americans show up to church 3 out of 8 Sundays."[21]

Why is this happening? If the world is slowly getting worse and more bad things are happening on the earth than ever before, why are people attending church less and less? Personally, I think there's so much shame still inside people that they'd rather stay at home than deal with it. Too many Christians are in such a condition that they can't come out and be truthful about things. You know; things that have happened to them. Bad situations of which they are ashamed and for which they really need deep healing. They are not finding the all-amazing transforming power of the love of God within our churches like they need to find. The fact is that *everybody has a story*; but Christians inside the church are just as bad sometimes as the people outside the church. We all want to hide our "stuff": our sin, shame, and insecurities. This is why the church is slowly dying in attendance while the "emotionally-charged protective movements" are often growing.

The freedom and deep relational values that are at the core of our Christian faith aren't there in the church the way they are supposed to be. That's what we're supposed to be inside our churches. It is only when you get to know someone's story that you can understand why they act a certain way in life. *Our relationships in the church need to be healed and our masks need to come off so that God can restore what needs to be restored.*

---

21. "9 Sobering Church Attendance Statistics," *Pro Church Tools*, September 7, 2018, accessed May 3, 2019, https://prochurchtools.com/9-sobering-church-attendance-statistics-ep-132/.

There's a great deal in the church, and the leadership isn't dealing with in these areas at all. My husband and I pastor a church. Believe me, I know. I see it every week. And what is happening week after week is that the "stuff" is just getting covered up. The church must rise up and start to truly heal from the inside out.

# Chapter 9: Healing the Bastard Curse

Concerning fatherlessness in America. One statement from Focus on the Family reads: "The numbers are staggering: 24 million children live without their biological father in the home. 24 million children—that's one out of every three children in the U.S. As huge as that number is, it doesn't tell the whole story about father absence. Due to separation and divorce, many of the children who lived with their fathers when these U.S. Census Bureau numbers came out, no longer do so."[22]

It is commonplace in our culture for most of the children who live in our communities to have a stepfather or no father at all—or, worse yet, they may have a father in the home who, instead of being protective and caring, is extremely violent or a drunk. These children might be subject to drug-fueled attacks or abuse committed in other ways. The absence of a loving father can be detrimental to a child. For a child without a father, this absence can be one of the toughest obstacles in life to overcome. Having no father, or a horrible father, around can affect a child for their entire life.

For you, the reader—potentially one who may not have a father figure in your life—God sees this and He understands.

---

22. "The High Cost of Fatherlessness: To All of Us," *Focus on the Family*, January 30, 2018, accessed May 3, 2019, https://www.focusonthefamily.com/socialissues/marriage/high-cost-of-fatherlessness/high-cost-of-fatherlessness-to-all-of-us.

But you, God, see the trouble of the afflicted; you consider their grief and take it in hand. The victims commit themselves to you; you are the helper of the fatherless. (Psalm 10:14)

A father to the fatherless, a defender of widows, is God in his holy dwelling. (Psalm 68:5)

## How the Bastard Curse Enters a Life

First of all, what is a bastard? The word *bastard* is defined as "born of parents not married to each other" or "an unpleasant or despicable person."[23]

The word doesn't sound like a good one. In our culture, it is a common curse word spoken against someone and is not used according to its actual meaning. Now that you know a lot about me and my family, I want to share the power of how God can work in a life beyond our mistakes in order to heal the next generation from the consequences of our own sin. This is what He did in my oldest son's life, the son I had not admitted was mine.

## God Can Heal a Person from the Bastard Curse

I want to share how the bastard curse worked in our family's life. When my oldest son, Jason, graduated from high school and went to college, he still felt that something was missing on the inside. Something was off, but he couldn't tell what. When my oldest son, Jason, returned home from college one year, he asked for prayer from a deliverance team that I was connected with at the time. During this prayer time, God dealt with "the bastard curse." In the prayer meeting, one of the leaders saw Susie's mother wiggle Jason's toes in the hospital and say, "You're

23. "Bastard," Google Search, accessed May 03, 2019, https://www.google.com/search?source=hp&ei=AkcmXIiIBYil_QaizrrADA&q=bastard definition&oq=bastard d&gs_l=psy-ab.1.0.0l10.1413.10563..13059...0.0..0.224.1097.5j3j1......0....1..gws-wiz.....0..0i131.VTgdU6LkodE.

a bastard." This opened the door for a curse to be assigned to Jason from a young age. This curse was able to torment Jason because he had been conceived outside of the marriage covenant. He was our first child, the one conceived through rape.

This spiritual battle began at his conception and the devil will use any legal right or violations to assign a curse to a person to stop their ability to walk in their God give inheritance in Christ Jesus.

The bastard curse will attack your inheritance and cause you to wander from place to place or try to work for your acceptance and approval all your life until the day it is broken. This is a demonic spirit that makes sure you never receive the Father's blessing. This was what was tormenting my firstborn son. It is that powerful!

During the prayer time, God revealed this to one of the individuals on the prayer team and me at the same time. The change for Jason, through this deliverance, was literally like from night to day. God broke that bastard spirit off him and the effects of it as well. From that day on, Jason and I became best friends. There had been an unseen barrier in our relationship.

## The Bastard Spirit

No one person is an expert on deliverance. I surely am not, but I have learned some things through this ordeal. This is how the bastard spirit works:

First of all, the bastard curse will cause someone to wander from place to place. This is especially true in church relationships. What kills a person who is attacked by the bastard spirit's relationships is the result of that person never being able to build healthy church relationships, because this spirit will constantly attempt to get them into a situation of rejection or force them to feel disconnected. Instead of being a "son" or "daughter," the person will feel like a stepchild that nobody wants. Sometimes the church does the same thing. This happens when we lead someone to get saved and make the church their savior instead of Father

God. This is why so many church-hop, looking for the true inheritance that only comes from the Father above.

Next, the bastard curse will also cause someone to miss their inheritance because a "bastard" in the natural has no inheritance. For this reason, the manifestation of this evil spirit will cause the person to severely lose out on many of the promises God has given to them. Their inheritances will be taken from them.

> A bastard shall not enter into the congregation of the Lord; even to his tenth generation shall he not enter into the congregation of the Lord. (Deuteronomy 23:2 KJV)

The good news is that if you detect that you or someone you love has this problem, the bastard spirit *has to submit* to the power of God's love. The bastard spirit will break with the blood of Jesus. Yes! It can break—and it will! When this spirit is broken, God returns the person's inheritance and His blessing. He puts deep roots into that person's life, and they become rooted more deeply than ever before. The Lord will then supernaturally return and restore the person's inheritance. The devil is a legalist—and he will use anything in his power to keep us from our true inheritance,

## The Bastard Spirit is a Breeding Ground for Rejection

One area that God will deal with at some point when this spirit is revealed is rejection. Rejection! Nobody likes it!

University of Michigan psychologist Ethan Kross, PhD, and colleagues scanned the brains of participants whose romantic partners had recently broken up with them. The brain regions associated with physical pain lit up as the participants viewed photographs of their exes."[24]

---

24. Kirsten Weir, "The Pain of Social Rejection," *Monitor on Psychology*, April 2012, accessed May 04, 2019, https://www.apa.org/monitor/2012/04/rejection.

Rejection is real and it will affect us. The connection between the absence of a loving father or mother in the home and rejection is not a problem the person experiences once in a while. It is not here today and gone tomorrow; instead, it can be progressive and long-term. The effects on the emotions and the brain just on short-term rejection has been proven through science and brain scans. Can you imagine the effects present through long-term, suppressed rejection from the person who was supposed to love and protect you the most and who was not around?

What has happened in our culture is that too many children are born without their biological fathers around. This has opened up a wave of innocent kids running around. Many of them don't even realize that they are dealing with rejection and a "bastard curse" that attacks them on a regular basis. I am not saying this is the case for every person who doesn't have or didn't have a father growing up. I know many great people who are doing fine without their fathers around, but this was not what God intended in the first place. When you have a father who isn't around because they chose not to be or, worse, you have a father who *is* around who wounds you, healing needs to happen.

## Israel and Four Hundred Years

The nation of Israel was with God, and then the people turned from God. They rebelled against Him; and then when God asked to have them back, they refused. This put the Israelites into slavery for four hundred years. Four hundred years is exactly ten generations. Ten generations is how long a bastard spirit can run in the bloodline.

I believe that this current generation is one of the largest generations ever that has had to deal with the plague of fatherlessness. Not one generation to now has had this many fatherless children on earth. For this reason, this is the one generation above every other that has the greatest potential for coming into contact with the Father's love at a level that all previous generations have not been able to encounter here in the United States.

Because of this and the curse of the bastard spirit, I am certain that this is one of the first generations that will have a legal right to genuine spiritual authority to walk into a double-portion mantle just like Elisha did. This is the result of them having to deal with the heart of abandonment at a level other generations never did, if they are open to receive this. They are set to receive the spiritual legal authority to claim their inheritance *and their roots*—both at the same time. If God can cause the Israelites to go into slavery for four hundred years for the sin of rejecting Him as a Father, how much more is He willing to bless a generation for accepting His love, the Father's love?

This current generation gets to claim both their spiritual inheritance from the spiritual parents (adopted parents) *and* the birth parents, from people who, in some cases, they have never even met. This is going to open the door for a double-portion blessing over their lives. This current generation will be able to walk in ways like none other before it.

## How Does This Apply to the Church?

Odds are that there are a lot of people walking in and out of our churches who don't have fathers or mothers with them. It's mostly the fathers that are missing too. A father will normally abandon a child long before a mother would ever consider doing that. If you want to see the power of unconditional love, just go near a mother when her child is in danger. It is like trying to take a cub from a mama bear.

Now let's apply this to the current state of the American church. Just as we can create a "bastard" in the natural through abandoning a person or forcing them to be rejected by those who are supposed to love and protect them the most, spiritually speaking, we can also create a "bastard" inside the church instead of fostering the idea of raising up true sons and daughters.

This is how we can do this:

When we set regulations over relationship, we unfortunately bind the heart of the person to those rules instead of releasing that person into their destiny. When we create church structures that people must serve instead of serving Jesus relationally, we bind them too. When people are expected to care for the needs of the church's leadership rather than the leadership serving the needs of the people, we do the same thing. In other words, the church should be equipping God's sheep and not using them for our own gain.

When we did this, we opened the sheep—God's people—to a slave mentality, or a bastard spirit. When it becomes obvious to a church attender that the leadership really wasn't there for them but instead was just using them for what they could get from them, this type of bondage was set into their life. We are binding the saints as slaves instead of releasing the children of God to claim their inheritance.

As a church, we must help our people discover how to walk into fullness. This means that we must help them break off things like the bastard curse. We must help them walk in their true inheritance instead of forced submission, which is just like Egypt's slavery.

It is time to set our children free! It is time to unlock the doors of the church and set our churches free. No more bastard curse.

Remember Joseph and how he was sold into slavery by his brothers? He was forced to be a slave. When Pharaoh put him into power, they put a robe on him, as well as a gold chain and a signet ring. What Joseph didn't change was his sandals. Joseph was still a slave, and thus the nation of Israel was reproduced as a slave to Pharaoh in Egypt because you always reproduce who you are. Like begets like. Joseph was a slave and did not have the freedom to leave. New sandals would have been a sign of his ability to leave—a sign of freedom. Now, connect this to the parable of the prodigal son. His father gave him a robe, a ring, *and his sandals.* The Prodigal Son chose to come back as a slave, but Father restored his sonship—and still gave him sandals with which to leave again if he chose to do so. If there isn't a choice, it's not true freedom.

> Then our sons in their youth will be like well-nurtured plants, and our daughters will be like pillars carved to adorn a palace. (Psalm 144:12)

# Chapter 10: The Power of Healing Through Accountability

## Healing Starts with Accountability

Accountability! We all use this word and many of us may assume that we are accountable. By the end of this chapter, you might be surprised to find that you may not be as accountable as you think.

What exactly is accountability? Well, let's start first with a definition so that we are both on the same page.

> *Accountability*: the fact or condition of being accountable; responsibility.[25]

Another way to understand this important Christian value is through the words of Charles Stanley: "An accountability partner is able to perceive what you can't see when blind spots and weaknesses block your vision. Such a person serves as a tool in God's hand to promote spiritual growth, and he or she watches out for your best interest."[26]

Accountability is that important! It is vital between you and God and it is important for you to be accountable with others too. Good men and women of God have morally fallen in this world because they were

---

25. "Accountability," Google Search, accessed May 04, 2019, https://www.google.com/search?client=firefox-b-1&q=accountability definition.

26. "Inspirational Words of Wisdom," *119 Accountability Quotes*, accessed May 04, 2019, https://www.wow4u.com/accountable-quotes/.

not accountable. When you listen to stories about how great pastors fell into sexual immorality—when it's all over and they share the truth about the matter—almost all of them will say that they "checked out" in one form or another. They got to a place where they were no longer accountable to anyone. They were at the church office, still visiting people, preaching great and powerful messages, and souls were getting saved; but something deep on the inside had shifted. They were no longer talking about their issues or love matters and, more than likely, things were going on at home that God didn't like. Sadly, during this time, this good pastor—this married couple—were both secretly placing all of their dirty laundry under the rug. After a long time, things toppled; someone bit the rotten apple of sexual sin, and down their marriage and church went. Meanwhile, their congregation sat there in shock as they heard the news: "The pastor has morally failed!"

Everything comes crashing down in a moment's time. A new pastor will eventually come in. The former pastor and his family will be forced to go into long-term marriage counseling that may take years to heal—perhaps a lifetime. Accountability is vital. Many will suggest, after the fact, that the sin could have been prevented had accountability been in place. Truly, the lack of true, genuine accountability destroyed that pastor and that congregation. Accountability is that important!

## Learning to Walk in Purity

The first thing that God gave me after our marriage was restored was three godly men to become my accountability partners in my spiritual life. This was part of the restoration process, so that I could be healed enough for God to trust me with a wife. This also included open range conversations about my emotions and my sex life. One of the guys lives in my neighborhood. We actually walk together just about every night through our neighborhood; his wife is on my board, and he is one of my best friends. Through the years, I have been able to share with him openly about topics like marriage, masturbation, struggles with pornography, and the many different frustrations that I have dealt with as we walk down the road of life together. True accountability is never one-sided. We need each other!

Accountability is important because when we get angry or something bad happens, we often shift that negative thought or energy to something that will only make matters worse. I did that! That was me! In the past, I would get mad and get angry; then I wanted to get drunk and get laid. This was my life for a long time before God dealt with me and fixed me on the inside. What we have to understand is that as bizarre as these thoughts of mine may appear to some, to others, these are real true emotions that they don't know how to handle. Some have suggested that for a man, having sex can be equivalent to getting high on a drug and as powerful in the brain as cocaine. There is also medical research that suggests that when a man ejaculates, the same two chemicals are released as those released when taking cocaine. If this is true, now do you understand why some men will stop at nothing to have sex? Men are visual. When we have an orgasm, what we look at during the time produces a memory that helps get that feeling. That's why a drug user runs to the same neighborhood and gets drugs and why men lust after women's bodies: it gives us the same high. See the connection?

## The Spirit of God in Accountability

So the first thing I did was get three guys and develop a relationship with them. In doing so, we became open and learned to pray with each other on a regular basis. Prayer—with people you trust—really does work; it can change the lives of those involved. During our talk times as men, we were open and honest with each other. To this day, we still are. I have learned to be outgoing and up front with my weaknesses with these guys because there is healing in doing so. When one person in the group is in trouble, we all try to pray and assist him in whatever way we can. There is accountability, but there is also strength in numbers. I am confident that if something serious happened to me or Susie, these men and their wives would be there for us in the best way possible. We need each other.

> Therefore, confess your sins [*faults and weaknesses*] to one another and pray for one another, that you may be healed.

111

> The prayer of a righteous person has great power as it is
> working. (James 5:16 ESV, addition and emphasis mine)

As my relationships grew with these three men, the Spirit of God would also work more through their lives. They began to hear the Spirit say things to them about me that I didn't know God was speaking to them about. For example, I would get mad at my wife, and within twenty-four hours all three of them would call me. (Anger was my trigger.) We gave the Holy Spirit permission to tell on each of us when one of us was weak. I willingly gave these three men permission to call me out when I was in the wrong. This is true accountability, and this is how someone walks through the healing process.

## Your Accountably Will Affect Your Spouse

As I grew closer to these men and their families, so did Susie and the other wives. Susie also picked up on this. It is one thing for you to be accountable with three guys who love you enough to tell you the truth when it hurts. It is another thing to have them openly tell the truth to your wife when she is brave enough to ask. Accountability can seem good but only be fake or superficial sometimes. I know a lot of ministers who are "accountable" because they are licensed through a church denomination. They claim to be accountable to another person, but they only see their district adviser once a month or maybe even four times a year. When they are together, they aren't talking about each other's sex life or what is really going on in their homes. Instead they are talking about the next ministry project that the district or the next big church in the area is working on. This isn't real accountability. It is institutionalism. What is happening, unfortunately, is that our institutionalized systems have eroded the concept of being accountable. I am thankful for the accountability partners God has given me.

## Accountability Isn't Accountability Unless It Has These Traits:

1. The person has a true relationship with you.

2. You deeply trust each other.

3. The group keeps private information private. (Never entrust your life to a gossiper.)

4. They are willing to confront you, no matter what.

5. The person will come find you if they need to do that.

6. You regularly meet and pray (weekly or more).

In my situation, my accountability friends were freely allowed to openly discuss truth with Susie too.

Susie knew my accountability people well. In the years when this group was still forming, she knew that if I was struggling with something or not handling life well for some reason, she could call one of my accountability men and talk openly to them. They knew this as well. So if I started to "check out" from the group for a while, my friends would call Susie and ask her how I was doing or what was going on. Likewise, if Susie noticed that I was wrestling with something, she would also call and talk to my partners openly just to make sure they knew what was going on. There is a direct connection between getting entangled in sin and disconnecting yourself with those in the body of Christ to whom you are relationally attached. When I started struggling with sexual sins like pornography, or being angry, or wanting to get drunk again, God dealt with me at multiple levels. He worked through my covenant friends and my wife to get me back on track. They all knew this then, and to this day they still do. They all know that if something is going wrong, they can interfere to get things going right again.

Today, if I am not doing well, it would be more due to business or church issues now and not the former sexual sins from my past. Even so, Susie will still call my guys and ask if I am communicating with them at all. And if they tell her yes, then she is at peace and she knows that it will all work out. If they tell her no, then that means they all now know I am hiding something or I am struggling deeply with something that is eating me up on the inside. When that happens, my guys come to the rescue. It is this level of trust and respect for each other that has built

Susie's confidence because she now has the ability to ask somebody else how I'm doing. She can enlist aid for me, and that is good.

## How Does This Apply to the Church?

> Then one of the elders said to me, "Do not weep! See, the Lion of the tribe of Judah, the Root of David, has triumphed. He is able to open the scroll and its seven seals." (Revelation 5:5)

Many people choose to make "sweet baby Jesus" out to be the fluffy and kind, plump King who will tickle your funny bone and make you feel good so you feel better about yourself. This is what many of our churches, and the messages behind our pulpits, have become nationwide. There isn't anything wrong with a good sermon that makes us all laugh, but when do we deal with the heart of the issues we grapple with daily? When do we look at the sin that is hiding within the camp? I am referring to your camp and mine! For me, I met the Lion of Judah, and God knew exactly what He was doing with me. With my personality and my brokenness at the time, I couldn't have handled a weak-kneed Jesus. If I had a coward for a King, it would have done nothing for me other than justify my abuse and my sin.

From the garage encounter, to the time Jesus walked into the bathroom to give me a robe of righteousness, all the way to the time He walked through the wall with bolts of lightning firing through the room, none of His dealings were weak. None of it had a shallow entry. I knew exactly who I was dealing with, and I respected Him from those moments on. That is what I needed. I was broken; I was abused, and then I got into pornography. During all of those times I needed something real, something that would change the course of my life forever. Something more powerful than the addiction of sex, drugs, alcohol, women, gambling, and pornography. All of this stuff was powerful, but Jesus showed Himself to be more powerful than them all.

This is the God I know. He is the One who will be there for me, standing with me when no one else will. My King and Lord gave me an encounter with Himself. This transformed my inner man and my mind. He changed the course of my life forever.

How does all of this affect the church? People come to church and get saved, and then the church places them into their system without providing any form of pure relationship. This doesn't create a walk with Jesus. Instead, it creates a walk with the church under the church regulations, structures, and terms, which often will not free the mind, will, and emotions. Normally, this process won't unlock the deep-seated abuse that must be released in order for a person to walk free in the Spirit. In the end, the church will fail to deliver the goods; and when the church fails, you have no walk with Jesus at all because it was supposed to be built around your walk with a local church and being rooted deeply with Christ first.

Too many times we're letting the church save the people instead of Christ Himself doing the inner work of salvation. In 1993 I was no longer surrendering to a church or to a system of the church; instead, I found Christ. When He showed up, He said I could either serve Him or hell would have its way with me. That was the end of the line for me. I met the King of Kings and the Lord of Lords, and I have been serving Him above and beyond any church system or structure ever since.

This is what the church needs! We need an overhaul of our systems. We need an encounter with God first and foremost above anything. We need to get back to the hosting part, the idea of hosting His presence in our lives, and not just serving the church through acts of kindness. We need to shift from less programs to a lot more of His presence in our lives. It starts with time with Him. There isn't another substitute.

# Chapter 11: Redeeming the Bride of Christ

U p to now, we have talked about my story, Susie's story, and some other real-life stories in the United States. Now we are going to shift to the central focus of redemption.

To do this, I want to tie together my initial abuse and lifestyle and Susie's heart for grace toward my life. While Susie was pregnant with Jason, our first child, she was praying for me, along with other people at a time in my life when basically I knew God but was still struggling with my relationship with Him. For instance, I had an encounter with God, but I didn't have a transformation because I didn't surrender all the way. I was living my life my way.

> The Lord says: "These people come near to me with their mouth and honor me with their lips, but their hearts are far from me. Their worship of me is based on merely human rules they have been taught." (Isaiah 29:13)

## Redemption Requires Surrender

Once I surrendered everything to God and made my life line up His way, not mine, it was only then that I could redeem my bride, Susie, the one I loved who I had led astray. I created the mess in my family and in Susie's life. I did it and nobody else. There comes a time that we have to stop pushing the blame off on everyone else. I could give lots of reasons why the mess that I created in my home was someone else's fault. I could blame my dad, the Sylvan Bishop family, or a whole number of people who I either thought had wronged me over the years or actually did. But God caught up with me on this and leveled the playing field. I couldn't hide and I couldn't run anymore. This is where true redemption begins: when we face reality from God's point of view.

## Learning to Heal and Learning to Grow

I had to redeem my own bride (Susie) first; and then He put a love for the bride of Christ in my heart. This true love is a real desire to see people set free, redeemed, and walking in the fullness of Christ. Here's the bottom line: I was completely broken, and I knew that under the right conditions I would cheat again. That's when God said to me, "You ever touch another woman wrongfully again and I'll kill you. Okay?" Then He promised to heal my marriage. And He did. He redeemed me and my wife.

Even though we were healed and growing stronger together, I was still afraid of failing again. When God threatened my death, it put the fear of God in me; but, looking back, this fear of God was really a season that gave me a window to get completely healed. Within seven years, the Lord had healed me and trusted me again with being around women, but that didn't mean that I trusted myself.

## Healing the Broken Ballerinas: The Fifty-Five-Year-Old Pastor's Wife

After the healing worked through my life and Susie's, we were both together in upstate New York with a group of people involved with ministry there. During this time, the Lord spoke to me and said, "I've anointed your hug. I need to heal that woman. Go give her a full hug, and I'll heal her on the inside." This was right in front of Susie and this woman's husband! In my mind, I was arguing with God. (Arguing with God doesn't work that way!) I didn't want to touch that woman. *A full-embrace hug! Are You kidding me, God?* But God always wins, and so I did it. For me, it was the most nonsexual and pure, intimate woman-hug

I'd ever had. And, as crazy as it sounds, the only way I can describe it is that my spirit man connected to her spirit. For the first time in my life since I was healed and Susie was healed, I got to witness the pureness of my physical body touch another woman's physical body through a physical, nonsexual hug. A pure hug. Then I watched the Lord fix this "broken ballerina"—this pastor's wife.

What happened to this woman was amazing. She was broken that night from many years of abuse when she was a child. I didn't know this at the time, but later she called me and shared her story of how God healed her abuse through that one single hug that God told me to give her. I was amazed at how God healed her broken spirit through a hug. Personally, I was petrified at the idea that God was using my hug to heal a woman on the inside. The Lord reminded me that years ago He had told me that one day I would become a healer to those who had been abused by the same kind of abuse I had once practiced myself. This was true redemption.

The next night I went to a Baptist church, and this time I saw a young blonde girl I had known for years. Once again, God told me to hug her to bring healing. Once again, He did not direct me to give her a side hug and a pat on the shoulder. I was supposed to give her a full-front embrace—the kind you share with someone you care for deeply. This was hard for me because I was still afraid of women. God told me He would kill me if I ever went too far with another woman, beside my wife, again. Knowing that this girl was young (only twenty-two at the time), I chose not to give her a hug as the Lord had instructed me. That night, I walked away from her and out of the church doors, defeated because I wouldn't do it. That night, Susie and I talked about this whole hugging ordeal and I realized that God was now entrusting me to heal *His bride* (the body of Christ). God knew that Susie, my bride, was now healed and trusted me. Most importantly, God trusted me. This was a major breakthrough for me that proved correct over time.

## The Broken Ballerina Dream (My Granddaughter)

Not knowing the full details and exactly what God was trying to say to me about all this, I went to Him in prayer and asked Him to explain it to me. What was really going on with all of this hugging stuff, anyway? While in prayer, God said, "I'll give you a dream tonight. And what you choose will determine if I use you in ministry anymore."

That night I had a dream about my granddaughter. At the time of this dream, my daughter-in-law was seven months pregnant with my soon-to-be-born granddaughter. In the dream, Madison was two-and-a-half and still in diapers. She was in a ballerina outfit, and together, we were walking in downtown DeLand, Florida (my hometown). All the store owners were talking to me, asking me how I was doing, as we were walking along. They were also commenting on how cute my granddaughter was: everybody loved my granddaughter. It was the greatest thing to have a dream like this. As the dream progressed, it got to about two o'clock in the afternoon and I had parked behind all the businesses. (At this location, you park downtown behind the street where there are apartments overlooking the parking lot.) I went to the car because my granddaughter needed a serious diaper change.

I put her on the back seat of the vehicle with the diaper bag. In the backseat, I had everything she needed to clean her messy pants. In the dream, I was standing near the back door with the door open with my granddaughter, and I was preparing to change her diaper and clean her up. As I did, I looked right up at the balcony of some apartments, and there were some people up there looking at us and watching what I was doing. I consciously made a decision *not* to clean her poopy pants! Even as I made that choice, I knew in my mind and my spirit that she would get diaper rash. I also knew my wife and daughter-in-law would never allow me to have my granddaughter alone again. Why? Because I did not take care of her and clean her up. In the dream, and still in the backseat of my car, I made that decision *not* to change her diaper!

Suddenly, I woke up and said to God, "That's not me. I'm not afraid of poop! I'm not afraid of this stuff! I go deer hunting and I am used to gross stuff, like blood and gutting deer." The Lord then said to me, "Son, you were not scared of the mess. You were afraid of the accusation of someone seeing you look at your granddaughter's nakedness."

In the dream, my fear was that if the people on the balcony saw me looking at her nakedness, then they would falsely accuse me of something of which I wasn't guilty. I was just trying to change my granddaughter's messy diaper. What God showed me was that I was still functioning in the fear of man. It was the fear of man that was still getting me to believe from time to time that God hadn't healed me of all my sexual sins; and therefore, Satan was using this stronghold to cause me to fear that I would have accusations brought against me if I did what God told me to do. For this reason, I was doing everything that I could to avoid any real-life accusation.

While I was processing this dream from the Lord, He said, "If you're unwilling to heal my girls, I will not use you at all." It became obvious that I was called to heal the broken ballerina, which represents the broken women of God in the church. God had healed me in order to heal what I used to abuse.

God's girls (His women) are a vital part of the body of Christ, and He's trying to put them in their rightful position. Right now, God is raising up people (men and women, young and old) to heal the women in the church, releasing the keys to the kingdom to them so the women of God could function the way they should. This is so real to me. I have actually been in services when God has caused me to see an angel in the service that was there to heal "the broken ballerinas" in that congregation where I was ministering. Not only is God healing the women of the church from sexual, mental, and emotional abuse, He is also healing the men of the church from the same thing. You see, the body of Christ is not reproducing kingdom offspring because we have given a hysterectomy to the bride and not allowed women to take their rightful place.

## Love Isn't Selective

When we are healed of sexual sins and insecurities, and then use the same healing power that Christ gave us, we can't be selective anymore with that power. Instead, we must be cautious with how we minister to other members of the body of Christ. When I minister to other women, Susie is right there with me, or someone else is and I tell Susie later. This is what helps keeps our ministry relationship and marriage pure.

## How Does This Apply to the Church?

People are getting abused by pastors and church leaders instead of being set free and redeemed. Remember, I had to go after my wife to redeem her. Christ went after His bride to redeem us too. There is a correlation here between church leadership and the body of Christ. What's happening is that we (pastors) are creating more broken ballerinas than we are healed ones! This is being done through the leadership of our churches, which is creating forced intimacy by requiring submission without any form of relationship. Any relationship that is forced without true consent and genuine relationship is rape. So, we have women coming into our churches each week and, unfortunately, we are offering them what someone else in the world offered them: date rape. We are giving them a Sunday morning date with us as we preach to them, telling them to line up, submit, and be what we want them to be; but we aren't offering any legitimate relationship with them. We aren't guiding them into what God wants them to be, which is the *fullness of Christ* and *not* the *fullness of our church systems*. This, my friends, is spiritual rape! People are getting abused by pastors and church leaders instead of being healed and nurtured, then properly released.

The answer to the problem of why thousands of churches are closing each year is simply because we (pastors) have created spiritual rape by creating submissive regulations without any form of spiritual intimacy with the people we shepherd. Christ is trying to redeem His church by pouring out His Father's love, and we are doing what Susie did when she was broken because of me and couldn't take it anymore. She took off and ran from it. It wasn't her fault she ran. It was my fault. She was running because she had never experienced true love from me.

The whole point of this book and the whole point of everything you have been reading ties into the fact that God is a Redeemer. He is a Restorer. He will restore us, even when we don't want to be restored. Believe it or not, sometimes the church is in such a state and sometimes the people of God are in such a condition that we don't even realize when Jesus is pouring out His Father's love. We don't even want it sometimes. God wants to pour out His love way more than we realize most of the time.

# Chapter 12: The Answer to the Me-Too Movement

The Me-Too movement has received a lot of media buzz over the past few years. But what exactly is its background? This organization started back in 2006 on a social media network. It was originated by Tarana Burke, when she was an adult sponsor and counselor with a group of young women at an overnight youth event. She and the team encouraged them to open up and share their emotions and feelings one specific night. As is normal, many shared typical teenage girl topics and concerns, while some talked in-depth about some really serious issues they were dealing with. One of the main topics, of course, was dating, sexual abuse, and other problems young women face today.

But it wasn't just that night that started this movement; it was what happened afterward. At the end of the evening, the counselors encouraged the young women to follow up with them, stay in touch, feel free to communicate further; but as normal, a lot of them didn't. They just moved on with life like the rest of us would.

However, one thirteen-year-old girl went back and wanted to talk with Tarana about something that had been bothering her. According to the Me-Too movement website, this girl, named Heaven, caught up with her after the youth event and began sharing her heart about what was going on in her home. She went on to tell Tarana that her mother's boyfriend was doing all kinds of sexual acts against her right there in her own home, and according to the site, these sexual abuses were so sickening that it took around five minutes for Tarana to stop the conversation and direct her to another counselor she felt could help her better. It was there, right there, that the look on that girl's face and her expression of rejection and hopelessness as she walked away, once again placing a mask on her face to hide herself from the world, caught Tarana's attention. It saddened Tarana so bad that she knew something had to change. This is where it all started.[27]

## Is God in the Me-Too Movement?

I believe that there is good in a lot of things that were started by people who may or may not have known the Lord at the time. I think this is the case for the Me-Too movement. I don't know a whole lot about the founder; I don't even know if she is born again. What I do know is that God is in the movement regardless. He is in this movement because it is allowing women to have an opportunity to release the fear, shame, frustration, anger, abuse, and rejection that has been placed on them through the overpowering actions of men. Men who were supposed to be there for them, to love, cherish, and respect them for who they were as a person, including their bodies. But these men did not do that. Instead of watching over them, they abused them. Instead of honoring them, they raped and harmed them. That is why God is using this movement right now. He is working through it in order to help women find release from what has been bottled up inside them for way too long.

On the other side of the spectrum, I also believe that this movement has taken a major political stance and that when we mingle politics and healing, unfortunately, politics will always highjack the healing part of it. You can find several cases across the nation where something needed to be addressed, and the political spirit took over and became a hindrance for true healing to take place. When politics become the driving force of a movement, it will have a DNA of revenge and not healing or redemption. We can get angry and revengeful all we want, but neither will heal the heart of the person. In my opinion, the Me-Too movement needs to be careful not to let a political agenda drive them away from their DNA of helping abused woman get healed.

---

27. Tarana Burke, "The Inception," *Me Too Movement*, accessed May 04, 2019, https:// metoomvmt.org/the-inception/.

I feel the Me-Too movement is a result of the "free sex" movement of the last century, which left women without the respect they deserve. So when societal norms swing too far in one direction, a "correction" takes place to get back to a more balanced area. As with all societal movements, there will be fallouts. But the Me-Too movement has given a voice to victims as well as a message to abusers that their actions will no longer be considered acceptable behavior.

## Is God Still Able to Work Through This Movement Now?

Yes! God is not limited to a political party, nor is He confined to what we believe He should be. He is working through this movement, just like He is constantly working through people who don't even know Him. Look at Cyrus in the Bible in Isaiah 45! God used Cyrus to ensure that the Jewish temple in Jerusalem would be rebuilt and that those Jewish people who wanted to return to their land for the purpose of building the temple could. Did you get that? God used a Persian king to rebuild the Jewish temple. If God can do this, He can do anything. And that is what He is going to do in the Me-Too movement. He is rebuilding lives.

Several years ago one of the female leaders in my church sat me down and challenged me because she felt like I was still abusive to Susie in certain areas. I listened to her and she gave me a lot of well-intended information about how I was wrong in different ways and how Susie was still being treated poorly sometimes. After she was finished talking to me, I said to her: "I see your point, but you don't really know me and Susie. We deal with stuff differently. We don't allow each other to get away with stuff that some couples might allow each other to do." I was just being honest. I don't put up with Susie's crap and she doesn't put up with mine. We tell each other up front what we are dealing with, and that is how we live. This keeps us right and honest with each other, but to some, this can come across the wrong way. However, it is our relationship and that is what works best for us.

Anyway, after she was done, I asked her how many times she had been married. She said more than three times; and so I asked her if she still talked with her former husbands. She said no, and then shared why she did not like her previous husbands and all the bad stuff they did. After she was finished, I offered this suggestion: "Try going back to the men that abused you and attempt to live out a relationship with them, regardless, and then we can talk further on this topic. You walked away, instead of through, those situations. Susie and I walked through it together, and this is what makes our relationship so strong and unique." Needless to say, she didn't have much to say after that.

The Me-Too movement is, at least, allowing women to have a channel through which they can walk their feelings and emotions out. This is something that is long-term for women and it takes a lot of effort, which this movement is allowing. So, before you go judging this movement for more than what it is supposed to be, think twice about it. I don't agree with everything that is going on in it, but heck! I am a pastor and I don't even agree with everything that goes on in my own church. Let's face it—we are all messed-up people, trying to get fixed the best way we can; and if an abused woman can get help through this movement because their church won't or can't help them, then so be it.

## In Reality, the Movement Is Pissed Off!

I believe the Me-Too movement is comprised of some really pissed-off women. Not all of them, but many, are angry at abusive leadership. Leaders in the government, Hollywood, businesses, and even in churches—and they are not taking it anymore. They are tired of going into interviews thinking that they have a chance to get a better raise or a better way of living, and all they get is an offer for sex or something like that in exchange for a raise. This has been going on for a long time behind closed doors, and I believe God is using this movement to address it.

Spiritually speaking, this movement is very similar, unfortunately, to Delilah in the Bible. In Judges 16, Delilah manipulated, set up, entrapped, and betrayed her husband, Samson, for money. If Samson wouldn't have been led by his unrighteous cravings, he would not have allowed Delilah and her influencers to take him down. Some of the accusations that are coming forward are in this same spirit. They are being sent out to destroy good men's lives—men who have done nothing wrong in the area of sexual misconduct. They are being framed. In some areas of the country now, it is so bad that some men won't even go out on dates with women anymore because if they yell "rape" or "abuse," everything comes crashing down on them without any grace on the matter. To make matters worse, the person accused is treated as guilty until he can somehow prove that he is innocent. Not everyone who is yelling rape was really raped. This is where evil political forces are coming into this system. Many are also lead by the same spirit that cries racism as soon as a person is questioned.

Not only is there a spirit of Delilah, there is also a murdering spirit that works through similar situations like those experienced by King David and Bathsheba. Bathsheba was innocent, and David had a three-day moment to repent and he did not; then he used his authority to have her husband killed. When we enter into sexual sins, it will end in some form of death if we don't repent. Unfortunately, these same spirits are out there today and they are both working through this movement. It's those two spirits that have come together and will no longer let this movement function the way it was in healing abused women. Political forces will always steal the agenda, and this political force is evil. It is an unholy alliance agenda that is manipulating hurt women, and this will only cause them to get angrier and not healed. That's the political spirits agenda: chaos!

## Walking Life Together Means You Must Change Together

When it is time to change for the better, you must change your behavior *together*. After the disaster I had created was over, Susie and I were walking strong with the Lord. We owned a lighting store together at the time. One day a lady called me from her cell phone and was ordering some food from the drive-thru window of a fast food restaurant. As she was ordering, I jokingly asked in the flirtatious tone that always got me in trouble, "Are you going to bring me some fries too?" Remember, I don't need a road map to find Stupid-ville; I can find it on my own!

When she came to the store, it was obvious that she was good looking and was acting as flirty as I had been on the phone. The problem was that she had some French fries with a pink ribbon tied around the box.

When Susie saw the fries with the bow, she flipped. She instantly came after me right in front of this customer. Susie asked, "Are we going back to this crap again?" The lady didn't know what was going on and was probably horrified. But I knew exactly what Susie meant. She was standing up to me and calling me out. Whether the lady with the fries considered it flirting or not, it could easily have come across that way. Susie caught it, picked up on it, and dealt with it on the spot—right there in the store for all to see. Needless to say, I caught on loud and clear about what Susie was doing and why she did it. I also realized that I couldn't live like that anymore. Coarse joking might be okay for some people, but not for me. In my case, it was crossing a line—especially when it was with another woman.

It was then that I realized that I had to walk at a stronger, more mature level with God and my wife. This is what I mean by saying that we had to learn to walk it out together, and we have to change together. Marriage is sacred, and it is sacred long-term. It is something that cannot be tampered with or serious consequences will result. The fact is, when your spouse feels uncomfortable with your lifestyle, comments, or jokes, then you need to change.

Which brings me to the next point: The answer to the Me-Too movement, or any movement for that matter, is the fact that:

## We Have to Go Higher to Guard Our Behavior

> Nor should there be obscenity, foolish talk or coarse joking, which are out of place, but rather thanksgiving. (Ephesians 5:4)

Basically, Ephesians tells us that we have to stop the foolish talk and use more control over our tongue. This doesn't mean that we can't have fun in life, and it doesn't imply that we have to be serious Christians all the time in order to be Christlike. It means we can have some fun—with pure, lighthearted jokes to lift the atmosphere of the people around us. But it says that when the jokes and conversations border topics and motives that are impure, this is not what God wants. The bottom line here is that if what we are saying throughout the day never contributes to the spiritual maturity of those around us, then we need a conversation change, or a direction shift within our hearts. This is what Susie was addressing. It was our marriage she was defending. There was still a wound there, and it needed to be protected.

> A fool's mouth lashes out with pride, but the lips of the
> wise protect them. (Proverbs 14:3)

As men of God, we have to go higher than where we have been in the past. We have to foster godly living within our homes and workplaces at all times. We have to make sure that we create an atmosphere that allows our wife and family to be nurtured and properly developed, instead of having to live in fear all the time.

Why are women lashing out all over the country? Because we men have not fostered them properly; instead we ignored them, suppressed them, and in many ways, abused them. This is why the Me-Too movement is gaining so much momentum. This (unfortunately) emotionally and sometimes politically-charged movement is harnessing all of the anger and frustration that women have dealt with for a long time, and they are channeling it against their abusers, the men who did them wrong. This will affect our country and our churches.

## The Miriams Are About to Stand Up and Confront Their Brothers

Miriam was Moses's sister and a prophetess and leader in Israel. I believe what is happening now will increase across America and other parts of the world, and the "Miriams" of our time will take a stand against the Moses-type leaders of our day. Moses was God's prophet to the people. Miriam was God's prophetess, just like Moses. In Exodus 7:1, God tells Moses that Aaron was to be Moses's prophet, and we also see in Numbers chapter 12 that Miriam is called a prophetess of the Lord. Unfortunately, she didn't handle her authority properly, but we must remember how God saw Miriam. God sent Miriam to His people to help lead them (Micah 6:4). She was called by God to be both a prophet and a leader to the people of God.

What is happening is that abused women are now standing up and saying that this is not going to happen anymore. It is going to stop. This will force some things to be dealt with in our governments and churches. Again, we think of Miriam, Moses's sister. Miriam was twelve years older than Moses. She was the one who put Moses in a basket and preserved his life. Though it didn't exactly work out well for Miriam, her stance, to some degree, was accurate. Moses was God's prophet, so everybody had most of their attention on him. Most would say that Miriam was rather rebellious, but Miriam was also telling Moses, "Hey, listen, little brother: you think you're the only one that can hear from God, but I'm also a prophetess of Gods. I heard God tell me to float your little butt down the river." Though that message didn't have the right motive at heart, it had a point to it. The Miriams are going to arise to help bring a better balance between true authority and proper respect and honor where honor is due. The Miriams of our time are the ones who are still floating the Moses-types down rivers to save their lives. They go out of their way, risking their lives, to help the kingdom advance, but they are often overlooked later.

On the flip side of this, the Miriams are going to arise and they will think that they can usurp the man of God because they helped him years ago or because they are older. I understand this, as I have three older sisters, and the bottom line is that it doesn't matter what God does through me: I was their "little brother Charlie" then and I still am now.

## Regardless, It Is Time to Rise!

Women, you play a very important role in the body of Christ. You're not just there to change diapers in the nursery or sweep the floors after everyone leaves. Though these responsibilities are important and someone has to do them, the church, as a whole, has neglected the needs of the women way too long. We have forced them into "church submission" without offering any kind of relational commitment to them. For the most part, I believe women have had it! They know that it is time to step forward and truly work on the Lord's behalf to lead the church.

The Miriams are going to start standing up to the Moses-type leaders of our time. This is already happening, but it will increase in frequency. For some, this is going to get really ugly because it will probably not be handled properly. For others, this is going to be the moment when God will show the men of God just how vital and important women are. This is also going to show the body of Christ just how much we have overlooked the power and presence of godly women.

### The Me-Too Movement from Susie's Perspective

As a person who was raped, I understand some of this. This is a movement that is allowing women to come out and tell their stories. It gives them the courage to come out and say it, share it, and not hide it anymore. They don't have to be ashamed of what happened to them earlier in their lives. But talking about it, pounding the ground, and expressing hatred toward the person who raped you will only bring you so far; and at the end of that trail, it will leave you empty.

Yeah, so you got to share what happened to you. Now what? What is next? Do you then need to go find them and make sure they are in jail forever? If they have passed, do you harass a family member who had nothing to do with it? Then what? Do you feel better now? Does this have to continue? It will! It will continue until you find forgiveness! It will continue until you learn to stop hating and learn to forgive. *Forgiveness* is the one thing the Me-Too movement can't offer you. It is only through forgiving that you can move on and find real peace.

The reality is that both sides need healing. Obviously the rapist has serious issues. Often, a rapist was also raped. Not all the time, but when you dig back into the lives of people who have a history of hurting others, they, too, were once seriously hurt and shattered as well. As malevolent as it may sound, the rapist needs to find forgiveness and healing for their past as well. Regardless of how evil you may think this person is, they still have access to God's forgiveness.

## How Does This Apply to the Church?

It's past time for the church to rise up and takes its proper place. It's time we allowed women the freedom to function the way that they are designed to be, and not the way we want them to be. We have spent too much time demanding this and that from women instead of nurturing and protecting them in order to allow God to mold them the way *He* wants them to be.

For many years we were taught in Ephesians 5:22 that women's number one role was to submit to her husband.

> Wives, submit yourselves unto your own husbands, as unto the Lord. (Ephesians 5:22 KJV)

What? That's it? So if a woman submits to her husband, then this is the image that God has of His church for her—just submission? If this is the case, then this is what is pleasing to God? Having women walk around and submit to their husbands all day out of fear that they might be a naughty girl and rebel, thus making God angry? Would He strike them down or something?

During Susie's time of torment because of me, she crossed out the word "submit" and placed the words "yield to love" in her Bible because she would not submit to an abuser but would only yield to a true lover and leader.

Doesn't sound like a lot of fun, does it? Nope! Men, put yourself in their shoes when you read this scripture or when you hear it preached behind pulpits. Personally, I think this is probably at the top of the list of the most misunderstood or manipulated scriptures of the Bible. Do you realize how many women have been verbally, mentally, and sexually abused over the word "submit"? Let's face it: every time some women have an argument with their husbands, they are no longer submitting.

Every time the man doesn't get his way, he throws out the "you-must-submit card" at his wife. No wonder women get so frustrated with men. This is not how it was supposed to be.

To me, it has always felt wrong, like we were missing something. It was like something that was being taught was hidden or out of place. The reason is because this isn't exactly what God was saying when it comes to the word *submission*. Let's take a look at another translation of this scripture. This is one of the few translations around that really draws out the truth about what God was trying to say regarding how a relationship between a woman and man can glorify Him.

> For wives, this means being supportive to your husbands like you are tenderly devoted to our Lord, for the husband provides leadership for the wife, just as Christ provides leadership for his church, as the Savior and Reviver of the body. In the same way the church is devoted to Christ, let the wives be devoted to their husbands in everything.

> And to the husbands, you are to demonstrate love for your wives with the same tender devotion that Christ demonstrated to us, his bride. For he died for us, sacrificing himself to make us holy and pure, cleansing us through the showering of the pure water of the Word of God. All that he does in us is designed to make us a mature church for his pleasure, until we become a source of praise to him—glorious and radiant, beautiful and holy, without fault or flaw. (Ephesians 5:22–27 TPT)

Notice the wording? Isn't that beautiful? It sounds more like a love story; it really depicts just how much Jesus really loved the church—so much that He was more than willing to die for us all. This sheds a different light on how a man and woman should relate to each other. The "submission" part is already a given. We don't have to be told over and over again to submit to authority, respect our parents, listen to our teachers, or pull over when a police car with lights on goes blazing by our cars. Why? We have common sense about all that. We follow through with these things naturally.

Ephesians speaks of how Christ loved the church and gave Himself for her. God told me that until I was willing to die for Susie, I would always want to kill her. My transformation as a husband began with my submission to Christ and resulted in my being willing to die for my bride. That was when true godly submission took place in my heart. In the early years of my restoration, I was frustrated with Susie and her stubbornness. Then the Lord showed me why there was no unity between us, and Ephesians 5:25 jumped off the page. "Husbands, love your wives, even as Christ loved the church and gave himself up for her." God asked me what He had done for His church. I answered, "You died for the church." Then He made this statement: "Charlie, until you're willing to die for Susie, the Enemy will always try to make you want to kill her." This total-surrender stuff was hard sometimes.

This is the same situation here. When Paul says, "Wives, submit to your husbands," he is really saying, "Wives, in the same way, be devoted (tenderly devoted) to your husband's life, just as Christ was tenderly devoted to the life of the church." Likewise, men, we are to be tenderly devoted to our wives. Love, depicted here, reflects the real image of what a family—and a church—should look like. When we love each other more than ourselves, we don't have to fight over who is in control. Instead, we walk together side-by-side, just like God formed us from the beginning.

The solution to the Me-Too movement is learning to walk in love above all else.

> Above all, love each other deeply, because love covers
> over a multitude of sins. (1 Peter 4:8)

# Conclusion: Last Thoughts

How do you sum up a topic like this? I have spent decades thinking about this moment, this time when God would have me share our story in a book with plain, upfront, undiluted honesty. Writing this information in a book has caused me to do a lot of soul searching. It has forced me to relive some memories that I would rather have forgotten. I have told many people what I am about to tell you—you know you have been healed or delivered of something when you can stand up in front of people and tell them something like this: "I once was addicted to pornography. Or I once was this, or that happened to me once."

That is the power of God's healing—when you are able to choose to never discuss the situation again or choose when to share it in order for others to find their own healing. One day the Lord said to me, "If you can't share your past, you are still attached to it."

## Our Battle Scars Are for Him

> "I have told you these things, so that in me you may have peace. In this world you will have trouble. But take heart! I have overcome the world." (John 16:33)

Our battle scars aren't meant to stay hidden. They are there to share in order for others to find recovery and hope. God has called you and me to walk in victory on this earth. This means that whatever the Enemy threw at us, we were able to overcome it by the power of Christ. When Christ left, He didn't leave us hanging down here. He left us to return for us, and in the meantime, He gave us His Holy Spirit to empower and guide us. As time progresses and we get older, this is where our victory is found. It isn't in the great things you and I accomplish while we are on this earth; instead, our victory is found in our ability to love the unlovable, forgive the unforgiveable, and trust in the most untrusting of circumstances. It's easy to build great things for God, but it isn't easy to walk in love when you want to hate with everything that is within you. When we lay these problems at the feet of Jesus, we find healing, and we find forgiveness. It is only here at the forgiving stage that we can show our scars. The scars are evidence of past things that tried to harm or kill us, but through Him we overcame. You will know when you are healed and it is time to share your story. When it is time, don't be ashamed of where you came from or what happened to you. Be willing to show your scars to heal someone else's wounds. I look at the Lord Jesus as my example; He would have had thousands of scars on His body from the terrible beatings He took. But after His resurrection, He made a personal visit to Thomas in John 20:25. He only showed Thomas the scars on His hands and His side. Jesus didn't have any scars after the resurrection— but He showed the scars that were needed for Thomas to believe.

With every important thing in life, there is a demarcation line. That is the case for me as well. There was a line of demarcation in my life, and it was when Jesus told me He was going to use me. The one who used to be the abuser was actually going to become the healer of the abused. Those words changed the course of my life forever. To get to this stage in life and to the point of writing this book has been a long, drawn-out journey, but it has been worth it in order to hopefully allow a greater level of healing in your life or the life of someone you love.

## Healing Is ALWAYS There!

God wants to heal you. He wants you to become the overcomer. It may take a long time or it can happen overnight, but God wants to heal you and cause the days of your life to be pure and right before Him, at peace with your past and future. I came to a crisis in my life when everything was falling apart, and that crisis was what led me to Jesus and recovery. It led to His restoration for my life. Out of His working in my life, I discovered that all along, the crisis was leading me to Him in order to bring me into His promises. God gave me these promises: I had a promise of a restored marriage. I had a promise that He would turn all this around in order to use it for ministry purposes. He has done both and then some. He has restored what I and some others once destroyed.

> "I will repay you for the years the locusts have eaten—
> the great locust and the young locust, the other locusts
> and the locust swarm—my great army that I sent among
> you." (Joel 2:25)

If you are a victim of rape or sexual abuse, *please* don't let it take another moment from your life. That is what Satan wants—he wants to destroy the best days of your life: the years ahead. However you have to get help, get it. There are many pastors and professional counselors out there who are more than willing to talk with you. In the same manner, I would like to hear from you as well. I am not a counselor, just a pastor down in Florida. Regardless, I am human: I screw things up, and I hurt and bleed just like you. You can find more about me and how to contact me in the back of this book or at my web address: www.charliecoker.com

# Appendix: Why Am I *Not* Ashamed?

He upholds the cause of the oppressed and gives food to
the hungry. The Lord sets prisoners free. (Psalm 146:7)

N
ow you have heard our story! You have walked through
some of the pages of life with Susie and me. You have seen
redemption in our lives and in the lives of others, but at some
point you probably had a question in the back of your mind, a question
that so many others have actually asked me about when they hear my
story. Obviously this isn't just another story about a walk in the park—it
is a story about the fact that I raped a young woman years ago. Not only
did I rape her, but I got her pregnant; later married her; had another
child; became a minister. Today we still pastor a church together, and I
also travel and speak on serious topics like what's in this book.

Does this sound bizarre or what? Something just doesn't fit though,
does it? Something has to be wrong; I mean, a former rapist is now a
pastor? How is that possible? God certainly can't use a former rapist,
right? How on earth does any of this tie together or work on any level?

Well, to be honest, it doesn't work. None of this works in the natural.
It can't, and it never will. It does work, however, when it is placed into
the hands of God. God has an amazing way of taking all of our messed-
up choices, our evil, our sin, and then shaking it all up and releasing it
back to us in a way that is restored, healed, and mended for life. I was
evil, but I am not now. How is this?

I found Christ and He came into my life. He forgave me of my sins and set me free from all of that evil and the nasty stuff that was in there, deep down inside of me. Only He can do something like this. Only He can take two broken people and put them back together in such a way that He calls us to be married again and pastors.

## Why Am I NOT Ashamed?

That answer is simple. The Charlie Coker who raped Susie over forty years ago isn't the same person who is writing now. I have the same body (but much older, more stretched, wrinkled, and banged up after all that time), but I don't have the same soul. My soul has been claimed by Jesus. I am a Christian now and I have been completely set free from my past. Society and the law teach that once you are a rapist that you're that for life. My story shows the opposite. My story tells the truth that sets us free! It is God's way of redeeming evil people back into a righteous kingdom.

Would I want to go back and erase that moment in my life? Yes. I can't do that, but God erased it by forgiving me. He changed me by removing the evil from me. All of us have something in our lives that we would have changed. For me, it would have been that moment, the moment I raped Susie. Would I have still married her? You bet I would! I just would have waited to have sex with her until *after* we got married instead of forcing it to happen beforehand. Bottom line: I can't change it, but God healed it. For this reason and for this reason alone, I am not ashamed. God did not call us to walk in shame. He called us to walk in His love.

> To you they cried out and were saved; in you they trusted
> and were not put to shame. (Psalm 22:5)

If you are reading this and you are an evil person—maybe you raped someone a long time ago, or maybe you raped someone recently—you need to give your life over to God. You need to surrender your life to Him. Secondly, you need to make it right. Walk it out like I did. It will be tough, and there will be serious consequences, but however you have to do it, do it! Let nothing stand before you and God on this earth. Let nothing stand before your clear conscience. However you have to get help, get it.

If you are reading this and you are a victim of rape or sexual abuse, remember that I was too. I was that young boy who was forced on the couch and raped by a teenager holding a sharp knife to my throat. I know what it is like to have your dignity stripped from you by force. I also know what goes through your mind and your emotions while you are recovering from a sexual assault. I believe that God can heal you. I believe that you can be free from any hate you harbor toward someone who did you wrong. God did that in my life. I am confident that He can do this for you too. I would also like to talk with you if you are a victim of sexual assault. My contact information is readily available. Feel free to e-mail me.

# Other Products by Charlie Coker

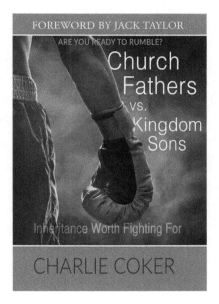

On the heels of being treated like an orphan by men of God whom he trusted—even his own father—Charlie Coker went into a vision that would change his life forever. In the vision he saw a gym full of boxers in training, sparring together and using various equipment to get ready to fight. On one wall was a poster of an upcoming bout that read "Church Fathers vs. Kingdom Sons."

This vision became the catalyst for Charlie's journey out of orphanhood to learning about the fatherhood of God and his own role in bringing healing and deliverance to the fatherless. Follow Charlie as he discovers an inheritance worth fighting for.

Find out more at www.charliecoker.com.

# Invite Charlie Coker to Speak

### Why Should You Invite Charlie to Speak In Your Church?

I have known Charlie Coker for over twenty years now and watched him grow in wisdom and in favor in his prophetic anointing in the most difficult testings of life's situations and circumstances. He is always overcoming and rising above as a champion for God and others, leading the way for many to discover their own identity, purpose, destiny, gifts, and talents. Charlie affords others a safe place of truth through relationship, wrapped beautifully in his uncanny way of loving people unconditionally while dealing with hard realities in order to see them mature and growing into all the things of Christ.

I love this man and his genuine, raw, authentic passion and delivery—both in word and deed. He is one of the rare ones you find in life who always show up, invest, and spur on and believe in you, even when you can't see it yourself.

— **Scott Lowmaster**
Senior Leader Journey Church, President and Founder of the Journey Center, Journey Academy, and the iMatter Foundation and Festival

Charlie can be contacted at Charlie@charliecoker.com  or by visiting www.charliecoker.com

# About the Author

Charlie and Susie Coker are founders of Identity Church in Deltona, Florida. They have also been in the lighting business for over forty years, concurrently pastoring and traveling in an itinerate ministry role, releasing the light of the Father's glory. They have been married for thirty-nine years and have two sons, Jason and Bryan, and five grandchildren.

Charlie and Susie have a unique ability to share the love of God and His healing power because they have walked through the restoration of a broken marriage and broken lives. They started as orphans, dependent on self-works for God's approval, and transitioned into sons of the Father. The guidance of Jack Taylor, their spiritual father, has been vital for this process. They are transparent about their struggles, and bring healing in many areas. Because of the training of the last twenty-five years, they are able to teach others how to rule and reign from a heavenly position.

Charlie's perspective and pursuit of the kingdom of God started in 1993 when King Jesus came to personally visit him. Jesus walked through a wall, asked Charlie to put his hand in His hand, and assured him that He would never leave or forsake him; telling Charlie that otherwise He was going to let hell have its way with him. This introduction to the King and His kingdom gives Charlie a unique insight into how the kingdom of God functions.

Charlie can be contacted at Charlie@charliecoker.com or by visiting www.charliecoker.com